America's "Failing" Schools

America's "Failing" Schools

Schools

How Parents and Teachers Can Cope With
No Child Left Behind

W. James Popham

RoutledgeFalmer
NEW YORK AND LONDON

KH

Published in 2004 by
RoutledgeFalmer
29 W 35th Street
New York, NY 10001
www.routledge-ny.com

Published in Great Britain by
RoutledgeFalmer
11 New Fetter Lane
London EC4P 4EE
www.routledge.co.uk

RoutledgeFalmer is an imprint of the Taylor & Francis Group.
Printed in the United States of America on acid-free paper.

10 9 8 7 6 5 4 3 2

Library of Congress Cataloging-in-Publication

    Popham, W. James
      America's "failing" schools : how parents and educators can cope with No Child Left Behind / W. James Popham
        p. cm.
      ISBN 0-415-94947-5 (alk. paper)
      1. Education--United States--Evaluation. 2. Education--Standards--United States. 3. United States. No Child Left Behind Act of 2001. I. Title.

LA217.2.P65 2004
371.1'58--dc22   2004041868

Contents

DEDICATION   vii

ACKNOWLEDGMENTS   ix

INTRODUCTION: SCHOOLS UNDER SCRUTINY   1

PART I. THE NO CHILD LEFT BEHIND ACT

1. A MAJOR EDUCATION LAW'S TESTING REQUIREMENTS   13

2. ADEQUATE YEARLY PROGRESS (AYP):
   LITTLE LETTERS, BIG IMPACT   21

3. REPORT CARDS AND SANCTIONS   37

PART II. EDUCATIONAL TESTS: THE HEART OF THE MATTER

4. SOME NUTS AND BOLTS OF EDUCATIONAL TESTING   49

5. MEASURING TEMPERATURE WITH A TABLESPOON   61

6. TODAY'S STANDARDS-BASED TESTS   75

7. INSTRUCTIONALLY SUPPORTIVE ACCOUNTABILITY TESTS   83

PART III. EVALUATING SCHOOLS

8.   THE EVIDENCE NEEDED TO EVALUATE SCHOOLS   95

9.   STUDENT AFFECT   105

10. DETERMINING A PARTICULAR SCHOOL'S QUALITY   117

CONCLUSION: WHAT TO DO NOW?   133

ADDITIONAL READING   153

NOTES   157

For my children, Shelby, Mitchell, Brent, and Christopher,
all of whom completed their entire educations in our nation's public schools.

Acknowledgments

To Catherine Bernard, tenacious editor, and Susan Arellano, vigilant agent, I am indebted for their insistence that I meaningfully massage what I had previously regarded as an altogether unflawed manuscript. Dolly Bulquerin, world-class word processor, also has my gratitude for making a legitimate manuscript out of my primitive scratchings on yellow pads of paper. I am once more grateful to Dr. Sarah J. Stanley, former public school teacher and principal, who remained married to me during another book's preparation. Finally, I am thankful to the many parents and public school educators who took the time to speak with me and thereby provide me with their reactions to our nation's new school evaluation law.

Introduction
Schools Under Scrutiny

This is a book about schools, good ones and bad ones. I wrote this book because school quality is important. It's especially important to the parents who currently have children in school and to the teachers who staff those schools.

Parents, of course, want their children to get a great education. No parent I know wants a child to go to an ineffective school. Similarly, teachers want to do a great job of instructing their students. No teacher I know wants to supply students with ineffective instruction. Yes, school quality is not only important now, but surely has been ever since schools arrived on the scene.

Yet a recently enacted federal law is forcing us to dramatically rethink our ideas about school evaluation. That law will soon cause thousands of U.S. schools to be labeled as "failing." Some of those schools will certainly deserve such a label; others won't. Moreover, some schools that are currently doing a second-rate instructional job won't even be identified as inadequate. If this sounds crazy, you'd better start getting used to it. A new school evaluation game has now arrived, and all of us need to learn its rules.

EVALUATING THREE FICTIONAL SCHOOLS

Let's get right into the determination of a school's quality. I'm going to describe three fictitious schools for you. I want you to read each of those three descriptions, and then decide which school, if any, should be regarded as a "failing" school.

School No. 1 is located in a fairly affluent Midwest suburb. Since it was first built, almost twenty years ago, this school's students have scored exceptionally well on the nationally standardized achievement tests administered each year to the eleventh graders in all three of the district's high schools. In April 2003, near the close of the school year, eleventh graders in this district were given, instead of the national tests, newly developed state tests that were "better aligned with the state's curriculum goals." School No. 1's students seem to be really loyal to their school, taking special delight on any occasion that their school outperforms the district's other two high schools—whether it be at football, basketball, track, or even test scores. So the parents of a sophomore student in School No. 1 were not surprised when their daughter announced at dinner that August, "Not only did our eleventh graders score well enough on last April's tests so we squashed the district's other two high schools, our school's scores were in the top 5 percent of all the state's high schools! And almost 90 percent of the school's eleventh graders took those April tests. We rule!"

School No. 2 is a middle school that is commonly referred to as an "inner city school." Its students are drawn from several low-income neighborhoods of a fairly large West Coast city. School No. 2's students are dominantly African American (56 percent) and Hispanic American (37 percent), with many of those Hispanic American students having arrived from Mexico and Central America only recently. There is substantial absenteeism in School No. 2, and its teachers often complain about the high degree of transience in the student population so that, as one teacher exclaimed, "You barely know who will be in your classes from one month to the next." Each year the school's seventh- and eighth-grade students take a series of state-administered mathematics and reading tests. To no one's surprise, School No. 2's students perform poorly on these tests—with many students earning scores several years below grade level.

School No. 3 is an elementary school serving a small southern town. For the past four years, School No. 3's principal, an extraordinarily energetic woman, has committed herself and her staff to "the elimination of any 'achievement gap' between our school's minority and majority students." As a result of the staff's efforts, on each of the spring achievement tests administered in recent years to the school's students in grades three, four, and five, differences in achievement test results between the school's majority and minority students have steadily been shrinking. On last spring's tests, in fact, with the only exception being some fairly low scores earned by about forty-five Vietnamese students whose families moved to town only a year ago, test score differences between School No. 3's majority and minority students were essentially nonexistent. When the school's principal announced those test results to the district superintendent with only mildly masked pride, she also pointed out that her school's students had "scored in the top 25 percent of all the state's elementary schools."

All right, you've had a chance to consider three fictitious schools that I've invented just to make a point. However, don't think for a moment that the three schools I've made up don't exist in real life. You'll find them all over America, and many people will be judging the quality of those schools in roughly the same way you just did.

Well, what's the verdict on these three schools? I suspect that most readers concluded that two of the schools were doing a pretty good job and one wasn't. A quick analysis suggests that Schools No. 1 and 3 were doing well, while School No. 2 wasn't. Maybe that would have been a sensible judgment a few years ago, but there's now a new federal school evaluation law on the books and, according to that law, *all three schools* would be considered "failing" schools. Let's see why.

School No. 1's achievement test scores were great, but less than 90 percent of the school's eleventh graders took the state's spring tests. Federal law now says that if at least 95 percent of a school's eligible students do not complete the state's annual achievement tests, the school automatically fails—no matter how high its test scores are.

For our "inner city" School No. 2, its sad story will be encountered far too often in most of the nation's urban settings. The school's low test scores would assuredly, new federal law or not, make any reasonable observer conclude that School No. 2 was not successful.

Turning to School No. 3, it seems impossible that the staff at this southern school would be regarded as anything other than superlative. The school's energetic principal seems to have her staff really rolling in a quest for "gap reduction." However, a provision in the nation's new school evaluation law requires that *all* minority groups earn sufficiently high test scores. So, even though the school's small group of Vietnamese children arrived little more than a year ago, their low test scores mean that the school must be designated as a failing school—despite the staff's otherwise marvelous efforts.

I hope you understand why I indicated a few paragraphs ago that a new federal school evaluation law is certain to shake up people's ideas about how our schools are to be judged. Let's turn, then, to that law and its more shake-inducing elements.

AN IMPORTANT FEDERAL LAW AND AN AVALANCHE OF FAILING SCHOOLS

On January 8, 2002, President George W. Bush signed into law the No Child Left Behind Act (NCLB). Technically, this legislation (Public Law 107-110) was one in a series of reauthorizations of the Elementary and Secondary Education Act (ESEA), a fund-filled federal law first passed in 1965. But this most recent reauthorization—that is, NCLB—incorporated a set of significant regulations regarding how to determine the instructional quality of America's schools. Putting it more directly, this federal law established new ground rules requiring the nation's public schools to be carefully evaluated in such a way that the quality of an individual school can be rigorously ascertained. Moreover, the results of those evaluations must, as decreed by this significant law, be relayed to parents and the general public in the form of school-focused report cards. That's right—report cards intended to grade *schools, not students.*

BY ANY OTHER NAME...

One of the consequences of NCLB, I'm sure, will be that throughout America we'll soon see a great variety of inventive labels pinned on schools that fail to measure up. For instance, be ready to encounter such labels as "low performing," "in need of improvement," "underachieving," "weak," "priority," "in need of corrective action," and so on. However, I'm going to use only one label for such schools in this book, and that label is "failing." You see, now according to federal law, the dominant determiner of whether a school is performing satisfactorily will be whether the school fails to meet annual required improvement levels in students' test scores. A school that fails to promote sufficient annual increases in students' test performances will be designated as "failing"—that is, failing to have satisfied its yearly progress requirements. Despite all sorts of attempts to soften the negativity of such evaluative labels, enormous numbers of the nation's parents are going to perceive that their children are attending "failing" schools. Similarly, huge numbers of our nation's educators are going to be told that they work in "failing" schools.

One of the goals of this book is to allow readers to question the legitimacy of this "failing" label. Let me put it bluntly: of the many schools that will be labeled "failing," some simply are not. Just as seriously, of the many schools that escape the "failing" label, some are doing an unsatisfactory instructional job. In short, just as it is tough to tell "what's in a book by its cover," it is equally difficult to tell whether a school is doing a good instructional job merely because the school has or hasn't been labeled "failing" according to the provisions of NCLB.

INTENDED AUDIENCES

I wrote this book for parents, teachers, and others who are concerned about the caliber of our public schools. Such individuals need to understand what's at stake when a school is labeled "failing." I hope this book will help parents evaluate whether, if their children are attending a "failing" school, that school really deserves such a label. Parents clearly don't want their children attending a subpar school.

I also hope that many educators will better understand the reasons that their effectiveness is often judged inaccurately. Without question, many of the nation's public school teachers will take some serious knocks because of NCLB. Often, those knocks will be undeserved. If schools are to be labeled winners or losers, educators need to know why those labels were applied and if they are accurate.

Finally, I would like the book to be read by educational decision makers who can influence the way that, in a given state, NCLB is implemented. As you'll soon discover, there are ways that state officials can carry out this federal law so that children benefit. Unfortunately, there are also ways that state officials can opt for implementation approaches that will accomplish precisely the opposite result. NCLB, if unwisely applied, will harm children—not help them.

Frankly, most of the teachers whom I know would like NCLB to disappear. Indeed, most teachers would prefer that there be no educational accountability laws at all—whether state or federal. That's because most teachers just want to do a good job at teaching their students. Teachers don't want to be deflected by any externally imposed requirements to raise students' scores on some sort of accountability test.

Yet the nation's demand for educational accountability simply isn't going to go away. Too many of our citizens, because they possess grave doubts about the quality of America's public schools, have directed their elected representatives to hold accountable those who operate these tax-supported schools. For educators, then, the challenge is not to try to do away with educational accountability laws. That would be wasted effort. Rather, the trick is to figure out how to make an accountability law such as NCLB work in a way that enhances, not erodes, educational quality.

The more of us—parents, educators, decision makers, and concerned citizens—who understand NCLB's potentials and its pitfalls, the more likely it is that we can actually influence state-level policies about how to implement this significant federal law. Rest assured that if a state's educational decision making is influenced by knowledgeable parents and educators, odds are that more sensible state-specific decisions will be made. Therefore, keep reading. You'll find that *you personally*, if you choose to do so, can make a meaningful difference in how this pivotal federal law works in your state. Later on, I'll explain how you just might pull that off.

THIS BOOK'S GOALS

Even before enactment of NCLB, the nation's teachers had been under substantial pressure to improve their students' performance. Because test scores were widely regarded as the most accurate measure of students' performance and, therefore, a measure of teachers' effectiveness, it was not surprising that all sorts of demands were made on America's teachers to boost those test scores. As we'll see later, this relentless pressure to increase students' test scores has led to a serious erosion of educational quality in many parts of the nation. Important curricular content has been tossed out. Many classrooms have been transformed into test preparation drill factories. In short, students often end up receiving a decisively lower-quality education because of a misguided reliance on inappropriate test score evidence about school quality. It is ironic that a test-based "remedy" originally installed to improve educational quality has had, in many settings, precisely the opposite effect.

All of these test-induced reductions in educational quality were present in America well before NCLB was signed into law by President Bush in early 2002. But the new federal law, however, has dramatically ratcheted up the pressures on American educators to boost students' test scores. Thus, the harmful test-triggered things going on in our schools prior to the law will—*if the law is unsoundly implemented*— become much more prevalent and far more harmful. In short, the law's impact, depending on the way that a state's educational decision makers try to satisfy its requirements, could be profoundly negative. Putting it another way, both parents and teachers may soon recognize that the caliber of a child's education may be appreciably undermined by certain provisions in NCLB. That's why, in the book's first three chapters, I'll try to explain the key elements of this influential law.

As you'll see, this law now calls for an intensified scrutiny of every public school in our nation. Indeed, report cards describing a school's quality must now be issued to students' parents each year. And the overridingly important factor in deciding a school's "grade" is to be the performance of that school's students on annually administered state achievement tests. It is the nature of these state-level tests that can transform NCLB into a law that will help or harm a state's children. According to this federal law, officials of each state are free to use whatever tests they choose in order to implement the law. As you'll learn in later chapters, if the wrong sorts of tests are selected for implementing the law in a particular state, then the students of that state will be attending schools almost certain to be mislabeled. Schools labeled as failing won't truly be underperforming. Conversely, schools not labeled as failing may actually be providing inadequate instruction. The whole school grading idea will founder because the wrong tests are being used to evaluate school quality.

How could it be that a state's policy makers would deliberately choose the wrong tests to satisfy this important federal law—especially if it's true that inappropriate tests can erode educational quality? Sadly, in some of our fifty states—probably in *most* of our fifty states—the wrong kinds of achievement tests will be selected to implement NCLB. Use of those inappropriate achievement tests will lead to improperly evaluated schools, to worsened classroom instruction, and, as a consequence, to a deterioration of educational quality for children.

To understand how we have come to this sorry situation, in the chapters that follow, my intention is to (1) alert you to key issues associated with the evaluation of school quality; (2) describe key elements of NCLB so that you understand why, if badly implemented, the law can reduce educational quality; (3) help you understand what sorts of achievement tests should or shouldn't be used to satisfy the law; and (4) show you how a particular school ought to be evaluated. Finally, I'll also encourage you to personally undertake corrective action, especially if your state's children are required to take achievement tests unsuitable for the evaluation of school quality.

A hefty portion of this book is going to deal with educational tests. I want you to know enough about such tests so that you can determine whether a state's schools are being evaluated using appropriate or inappropriate tests. Clearly, if you are a parent of a school-age child, and your state's officials have opted to use *appropriate* tests to implement NCLB, then it's likely you will receive a school-focused report card that accurately portrays the quality of your child's school. In the same way, if you are teacher in a school that has been evaluated on the basis of *appropriate* tests, then odds are that your school has been accurately evaluated. However, if *inappropriate* tests have been used to implement this important law, then you really can't have all that much faith in the accuracy of any report evaluating a school. Thus, it's critical for you to be able to recognize the difference between tests that are appropriate and those that are not.

Educational testing is often thought to be such a technical arena that only a small group of quantitatively capable specialists can understand it. This widely held view is quite wrong. Certainly, there are particular details about educational testing that everyone doesn't want to know or doesn't need to know. Yet the chief elements of educational testing are readily understandable to just about anyone. In chapter 4, I'll review a handful of fundamentals about educational testing. Once you understand this modest collection of test-related truths, you'll be better equipped to know whether your state's schools are being properly evaluated.

Even if the right tests are being used, there's more to an accurate evaluation of a school than just looking at students' test scores. What I'll try do, in the last part of this book, is show you how a specific school can be properly appraised using various sources of evidence. School evaluation is tough. Moreover, it takes clearheaded people who are willing to be guided by appropriate kinds of evaluative evidence. But accurate school evaluations are surely indispensable if we want to make sure that America's children are well educated.

WHAT TO DO NEXT?

Throughout this book, I hope to clarify the issues surrounding the implementation of NCLB. However, I am warning you up front that at the book's conclusion I intend to engage in a serious attempt to persuade you, once you've looked at these issues closely, to take action. The reason that I'm going to entreat you to take action, if you find your state's schools are being evaluated with the wrong sorts of tests, is straightforward: if improper evaluation is allowed to continue, then your state's children will end up badly educated, and that's unacceptable.

Although in the past two decades there have been many instances of inappropriate tests lowering educational quality, the passage of NCLB has dramatically increased the likelihood of test-induced educational harm. Previously, many thousands of our nation's children experienced lower-quality educations because of unsound tests. Now, a significant federal law, if poorly implemented, can lower educational quality for millions of our nation's children.

That's why educators and parents need to find out what sort of state-wide testing is going on in their state's schools. If this important federal law is going to achieve its intended goal of enhancing the quality of U.S. education, the right tests definitely must be used. If the wrong kinds of tests are being used, then it is imperative that parents, grandparents, educators, and every other citizen find this out so that they can do something about it.

Let's turn, then, to NCLB and its implications for America's public schools.

PART I

The No Child
Left Behind Act

1

A Major Education Law's
Testing Requirements

Overwhelmingly passed by both houses of the U.S. Congress in late 2001, a significant federal education statute was signed into law by President George W. Bush in January 2002. The substantial bipartisan congressional support that this legislation enjoyed was surely due to the strong advocacy of test-based educational accountability previously registered by both Republican and Democratic candidates in their presidential campaigns. During the run-up to the election of 2000, both Al Gore and George W. Bush had often voiced their belief that the nation's public schools needed some sort of rigorous accountability system that relied on an expanded use of educational tests. Although there were certainly differences between the positions of the two presidential candidates, the cornerstone of both approaches to improving our schools was a marked increase in the use of achievement tests for students.

The underlying idea expressed by both Bush and Gore was that our public schools should be required to provide hard evidence, primarily in the form of students' test scores, demonstrating whether those schools were doing a good job. The two candidates concurred that schools in which students' test scores were low should be placed on some sort of improvement track. Given the substantial overlap regarding the school improvement remedies in the two parties' campaign rhetoric, bipartisan congressional support for the educational legislation that ultimately became the No Child Left Behind Act (NCLB) was present almost immediately after the year 2000 elections were concluded.

THE LAW

One of the most striking features of this federal law was its requirement for greatly expanded student testing. NCLB is a lengthy act, about a thousand pages long. But only a few parts of it really bear on the determination of a school's quality, and almost all of those parts are linked to the law's new testing requirements.

As I mentioned in the book's introduction, NCLB is actually the most recent reauthorization of the Elementary and Secondary Education Act (ESEA) initially passed by Congress in 1965. ESEA was the first federal statute that (as part of President Lyndon Johnson's "Great Society" program) provided really substantial, precedent-setting amount of federal money to local schools so that better education could be provided to historically underserved student groups such as minority and low income students. Prior to 1965, almost all funds for operating our public schools had come from local tax dollars. You'll sometimes encounter educators who'll refer to NCLB simply as ESEA, or even as "Title I of ESEA" because that particular section of the law is designed to help schools serving disadvantaged students and, as a consequence, provides most of the law's funds. Title I of ESEA has, historically, also contained the most constraints about how these federal dollars should be spent by the nation's educators.

Recent federal lawmakers, following the lead of their 1965 predecessors, have sent forth a clear message to the nation's educators: "We have ample federal money to send your way, but in order to get that money, you must follow the new rules that we've established." Given the substantial amounts of money that states and districts can collect from NCLB, most local educators—sometimes with clenched teeth—have agreed to play by the rules that will provide their schools with federal greenbacks.

Accountability/Assessment Provisions

The most important sections of NCLB that bear on the determination of failing schools are those parts of the law referring to *accountability* and *assessment*. Let's take a brief look at the meaning of those two important terms.

The *accountability* sections of the new law refer to those parts of the legislation intended to hold public school educators directly responsible for the effectiveness of their instructional efforts. In other words, in NCLB there are provisions designed to assure our nation's citizens that the individuals operating America's tax-supported public schools will provide credible evidence of their effectiveness. Based on such evidence, therefore, public school educators can be held genuinely accountable for the quality of the instruction they deliver to students.

Assessment, on the other hand, is simply a ritzy word for *test*, and these days we find most educators preferring to use the former term over the latter. The main reason for their preference is that when most people (educators included) hear the word *test*, they immediately think of the sorts of paper-and-pencil tests that they personally encountered when they were students in school. *Assessment*, on the other hand, is currently regarded as a label describing a much wider range of ways to measure students' performances.

For example, when educators refer to assessment these days, they might be thinking of (1) a student's ability to make an effective oral presentation in a speech class; (2) a collection of a student's best essays in an English class; or (3) a portfolio of a student's watercolors in an art class. The term *assessment*, therefore, conveys a broader conception of measurement than merely paper-and-pencil tests. In fact, *measurement* is simply another, slightly more technical synonym for assessment and testing.

Let's turn, then, to several of NCLB's key assessment and accountability provisions. In my estimate, there are three elements of this law that will lead to the wholesale identification of "failing" schools. The first of these elements deals with the law's requirement for new tests.

Newly Required Tests

While we will look at these tests in greater details later, there are a few fundamentals to be considered here. NCLB calls for all states to install annual reading and mathematics tests in grades three through eight, and one-time reading and mathematics tests in grades ten, eleven, or twelve no later than the 2005–6 school year. All together, then, NCLB requires states to test students at seven grade levels rather than only three grade levels, as was called for by the previous 1994 reauthorization of ESEA. That's more than twice the amount of required testing called for by previous federal law.

Starting in the 2007–8 school year, states must also administer science tests at least once in grades three through five, six through nine, and ten through twelve. All of the tests in reading, mathematics, and science are supposed to be the same for all of the state's students. In other words, the tests must be standardized. And according to NCLB, these state-administered assessments should supply accurate information about the specific instructional needs of students. In short, the tests should be diagnostic, providing relevant details about weaknesses in the students' mastery of what was supposed to be learned.

Returning to the reading and math tests for a moment, the law's requirement to test students at every grade, in grades three through eight, offers state educators a tremendous opportunity to identify a carefully considered set of increasingly more demanding math and reading skills to be assessed.

Those carefully articulated state assessment targets (and, therefore, the state's instructional targets), can identify a state's chief educational goals in these two key curricular areas much more sensibly and systematically than is currently the case in many states where state-level assessment in elementary schools often takes place at only two or three grade levels.

A few states already administer statewide tests at most or all grade levels. These states are the exceptions, however, so they will be less likely to benefit from the careful sequencing of instructional/assessment targets for grades three though eight in reading and mathematics. That's because, in the main, those states' educators will have already attempted to do precisely that sort of grade-to-grade sequencing of content when they began using state tests at each grade level.

NCLB tests are, by law, intended to measure a state's *curriculum* —namely, the knowledge and skills that students in a given state are supposed to learn. Because the determination of what's to be taught in America's public schools is each state's decision rather than a federal one, and because different states' curricular targets often vary to some extent, this means that there might well be substantial differences in NCLB-required tests used in different states. However, based on my personal review of many states' curricular aims in reading and mathematics, there is substantial overlap with respect to what's to be learned by children in those two subject areas. Some differences will occasionally be encountered from state to state, but in reading and mathematics, educators in different states usually want kids to learn pretty much the same sorts of things.

The specific tests to be used in satisfying NCLB are also left up to the states. Indeed, if a state wants to add a writing test to its reading tests, thereby transforming those tests into "language arts tests," that's permissible according to the law. The new tests are referred to in the law as *academic assessments*, and the only proviso in the law is that these tests address the "breadth and depth" of a state's "challenging" curricular aims. Although, as noted above, a few states have already been administering statewide student tests at all the grade levels now called for in NCLB, the bulk of our states will have to gear up for substantially more testing in order to meet the 2005–6 school-year deadline for NCLB's assessments for grades three through eight.

One Size Must Fit All—Usually

The tests called for in the new law are to be *standardized* statewide tests—that is, the same tests are to be administered to all the state's students in the same way. The federal regulations for implementing the law allow for a state to supplant a statewide test with local tests (for instance, to use tests devised in a state's individual school districts). However, such local tests, according to the law, need to be technically equivalent to one another; for instance, the local tests must represent an equally difficult challenge for students regardless of which district's tests are being taken. As a practical matter, that sort of technical equivalence is almost impossible to attain for a collection of locally developed assessments. It's difficult enough for a state to come up with *one* really good test—after drawing on the state's considerable technical and financial resources. For an individual school district to create seven grades' worth of good tests—and do such test development in a way that its tests are genuinely equivalent to the tests used in the state's other districts—would be a minor miracle. Thus, NCLB's assessment requirements are, miracles notwithstanding, most likely to be satisfied via statewide tests.

To my considerable surprise, the federal officials who oversee the implementation of NCLB have permitted a few states—Nebraska, for example—to satisfy the law's testing requirements using district-developed assessments. It appears that sufficient support for local assessment was marshaled in those states so that federal personnel relaxed their demands for standardized NCLB assessments. Nonetheless, it appears that local NCLB assessments will surely be the exception, not the rule.

Federal regulations for implementing the new law allow for students who suffer from severe mental disabilities to be tested with *alternate* assessments—that is, modified tests intended to assess alternate state-designated curricular aims. Yet a state is allowed to give such alternate assessment to no more than *1 percent* of its total students, which, of course, is a mighty small number. What this boils down to is, simply, that nearly every child in a grade level where tests are required (that is, annually in grades three through eight and once in grades ten through twelve) will be taking the same NCLB state-administered tests.

As you can calculate, if a state finds that 2 percent of its students have severe cognitive deficits, then half of those students will be required to take the regular NCLB tests. Not surprisingly, most parents of those children are concerned by this regulation.

The 2005–6 School Year as the Target

As indicated earlier, NCLB calls for the installation of these new reading and math tests no later than the 2005–6 school year. That sort of lag time was necessary because states needed to figure out just what sorts of academic assessments they would be using to satisfy the law. Moreover, because a number of states will choose to build brand new assessments that mesh more appropriately with their state's curricular aims, there must be ample time available for constructing such tests. Experience indicates that it typically takes two or three years to build the kinds of academic assessments called for in NCLB, so the delay between the law's enactment in early 2002 and the first required administration of the tests in the 2005–6 school year allows for sufficient test development time. Realistically, the new tests need not be administered to students until the close of the 2005–6 school year—say, in April or May of 2006. That's sufficient time to create high-quality new tests if, of course, states actually embarked on this test-development activity soon after the law's enactment. (As is all too predictable, many states did not.)

In the meantime, before the new academic assessments are initially administered, states are being allowed to use whatever tests were in place (and at whatever grade levels were being assessed) when NCLB was enacted. In the previous 1994 version of the ESEA, states were required to test students in schools receiving Title I funds at least once in grades three through five, six through nine, and ten through twelve. Thus, states typically chose to assess their students with statewide tests at least once in each of those three grade ranges.

So, in a sense, many states will be in a holding pattern for a few years, satisfying certain provisions of NCLB with existing state assessments, while moving toward full compliance with the law by testing, as now stipulated, substantially more grade levels.

AN OPPORTUNITY—TO WIN OR TO LOSE

One of the major points I'll make throughout this book is that the defensibility of any evaluation of a school's quality via students' test performances is almost completely dependent on the nature of the tests being used.

If I'm correct, then NCLB gives every state a marvelous opportunity to install statewide tests that provide accurate evidence of school quality and, therefore, can contribute to improving educational quality for the state's students. Appropriate statewide tests make it possible for parents to arrive at accurate judgments about whether their children are attending a high- or low-quality school, and such tests also provide educators with accurate evidence regarding how well they are doing. That's what we all want.

We are entering an era in which test-based evidence of school quality will play the key role in shaping parents' perceptions regarding the excellence of their children's schools. Obviously, the wrong tests will deliver the wrong evidence and, as a consequence, parents won't be able to get an accurate fix on how good their children's schools truly are. Nor will teachers find out how effective their instruction truly is. Depending on whether a state's educational decision makers choose the right kinds of achievement tests to satisfy NCLB, this precedent-setting federal law can contribute to the improvement or deterioration of a state's public schools.

We will take a look in later chapters at what kinds of state achievement tests are winners and what kinds are losers. In the meantime, we need to consider another significant part of NCLB intended to determine whether a school's students are making enough progress each year.

2

Adequate Yearly Progress (AYP)
Little Letters, Big Impact

In addition to the demand for expanded testing, a three-letter acronym linked to NCLB is almost certain to dominate the nation's educational landscape for the next few years. The acronym—AYP—stands for *adequate yearly progress*, and it is this particular feature of the new law that will lead to the labeling of schools (and school districts) as failing. You need to know why these three seemingly harmless letters will be sure to cause such a commotion.

AN OLD REQUIREMENT, NOW TIGHTENED

Actually, the notion of AYP has been around for a while. That's because in the previous (1994) reauthorization of the ESEA, there was a requirement that "Title I schools" (those getting ESEA Title I dollars) must demonstrate annually that their students were making adequate yearly progress. These Title I schools serve substantial numbers of economically disadvantaged students and, therefore, receive a great deal of the ESEA money specifically intended to improve the educational experiences provided to such disadvantaged youngsters. Title I schools needed to provide evidence each year (via AYP data) that such historically underserved students were actually benefiting from the federal ESEA funds awarded to ensure ongoing support for instructional programs aimed at the student groups specified in the law.

However, the *size* of the required AYP—that is, the annual improvements called for in the 1994 ESEA reauthorization—was left to the determination of each state. And because educational policy makers in most states were reluctant to set particularly demanding AYP expectations for their state (fearing that many of the state's schools might be unable to meet those expectations), a number of states established AYP targets that were absolutely trifling. It was not unusual to see state-level policy makers decreeing that their state's Title I schools should show a *2 percent* improvement in students' test scores each year. The lower the hurdle, of course, the easier it is to be a successful hurdle hopper. AYP expectations based on the 1994 version of ESEA were, in most instances, laughably low. (A 2 percent annual improvement in students' test scores would normally take place merely because a state's teachers, having become familiar with the items on a state's ESEA tests, understandably incorporated the content of such items into their next year's lessons.)

One suspects that when federal lawmakers, after the 2000 presidential elections, began to work on the ESEA reauthorization, they were aware of the trivial AYP expectations that had been established by most states to satisfy the 1994 ESEA regulations. And, it seems, those federal legislators set out to devise a way to outfox sometimes slippery state-level education officials. As a consequence, NCLB contains a set of far more constraining AYP regulations. This 2002 federal law has transformed ESEA's annual yearly progress requirements, at least in the view of our nation's educators, from a minor distraction into a major dilemma.

Let's see how NCLB's new AYP requirements work. As you'll discover, most schools will soon be labeled as failures primarily because they will have fallen short of attaining their school's annual AYP improvement targets. First, however, because the overall thrust of NCLB hinges so heavily on one key concept, let me briefly discuss the idea that *no* child, *not even one*, can be left behind.

One Hundred Percent Proficiency

Anyone who's ever been a public school teacher (and I was, once upon a time, a teacher in an Oregon high school) knows that not every single child is likely to be successful in school. Teachers would love to see all children sail through school successfully, but stories of academic success for each and every child—all across the nation—are best regarded as fantasy rather than reality. For a variety of reasons, not every single child will swim successfully through our public schools' sometimes choppy seas.

That's not to say that our public school teachers don't try—and often heroically—to ensure that all their students have a successful and rewarding experience in school. Yet the simple truth is that a proportion of students, and one hopes it is a small proportion, will not end up having a triumphant school experience. Politically, however, imagine the repercussions if federal lawmakers had come up with an ESEA reauthorization entitled Only Five Percent of Children Left Behind. Indeed the political rhetoric, of necessity, had to focus on the notion that *every* child could be successful, despite the reality that some children surely wouldn't be. By sending a *no*-child-left-behind message to the nation's educators, architects of NCLB were trying to remind those educators that they needed to do their very best to get as many students as humanly possible to succeed in school. Ideally, based on that aspiration, there would be darn few students left behind.

Given this motivation, those congressional legislators who crafted NCLB wrote into the law a requirement that, within twelve years from the end of the 2001–2 school year, a full 100 percent of the nation's students had to be "proficient." As you'll soon see, it is the resulting annual AYP targets based on that lofty but politically crafted aspiration that will soon lead to a widespread application of "failing" labels for tons of U.S. schools and districts.

Proficiency—A Closer Look

If NCLB says that 100 percent of our students need to be "proficient" within twelve years, what does this really mean? Well, the law requires each state to clearly describe at least three levels of student achievement—namely, *basic*, *proficient*, and *advanced*. These levels are referred to in the law as "academic achievement standards." A state can have more levels if it chooses to, but at least these three academic achievement standards must be present. And whether a student is identified as basic, proficient, or advanced depends almost exclusively on the way that the student performs on NCLB-required statewide tests described in the previous chapter.

States are permitted to determine the nature of student performance on state tests that define these three academic achievement standards. So, for example, a state might decide that on its math tests for grades three through eight, students' performances would be classified as follows.

Academic Achievement Standard (Performance Level)	Percent of Test Items Answered Correctly by the Student
Advanced	90 and above
Proficient	70 to 89
Basic	69 and below

Illustrative, test-based performance levels.

As noted, some states employ additional achievement levels, such as "below basic," but the law requires these three levels at a minimum. So, when NCLB says that in twelve years all students must be proficient or better, this means that in a dozen years (starting with the 2002–3 school year) all of a state's students, based chiefly on their performances on the state's NCLB tests, will have earned scores that allow those students to be classified as either proficient or advanced. The twelve-year target for every student to be proficient, then, is to be the 2013–14 school year.

Furthermore, in an attempt to oblige the nation's educators to attend more carefully to several often underserved student groups, in addition to the cumulative AYP targets, the law calls for test scores to be separated (disaggregated) according to students who are (1) economically disadvantaged; (2) from major racial and ethnic groups; (3) disabled; or (4) with limited proficiency in English. NCLB also calls for 100 percent of these four subgroups to attain proficient-or-above status within twelve years.

As you'll soon see, because the satisfactory performance of a state's schools depends directly on the difficulty levels of state-set academic achievement standards—that is, the state's chosen performance levels—there are already reports that some states, fearing an onslaught of failing schools, have revised their expectations of students (or, putting it more frankly, have lowered their standards) so that fewer school failures will be seen.[1]

Clearly, then, the two most important factors that will determine how many schools in a state will be classified as failures are (1) how tough the state-selected NCLB tests actually are and (2) the difficulty levels that are set for the state-determined definitions of *basic, proficient,* and *advanced.*

One thing that parents and teachers need to be on watch for is whether their own state's NCLB-related requirements have been deliberately watered down so as to avoid a public perception of educator ineffectiveness. Watered-down expectations of educators, of course, will often be transformed into watered-down expectations of students. And that's surely not what we want.[2]

SNARING THE SLIPPERY

I vividly recall my initial reading of NCLB. The bill had just been approved by a congressional conference committee in late 2001—several weeks before President Bush's signature was affixed to it. I was reviewing the section of the bill regarding AYP, and I saw that states were to be allowed to set their own timelines for moving 100 percent of their students from (1) where they were at the start of the 2002–3 school year to (2) a 100 percent proficient-or-better goal in twelve years. According to the bill, the first AYP increment was to occur in two years or less, and then at least in three-year increments after that. I saw that a state-determined AYP timeline was to establish these increments for schools' annual AYP improvements, but then I noted that these intermediate goals were to "increase in equal increments over the period covered by the State's timeline." When I saw the word *equal,* I realized what was going on with this soon-to-be-enacted legislation.

Federal lawmakers wanted school improvement, and lots of it. But they'd seen, earlier, that many of the nation's education officials had dodged the 1994 ESEA's requirements for AYP by trivializing the size of their state's AYP increments. So, unwilling to be conned again, congressional lawmakers essentially were saying, "Okay, states, you can set your own timelines for getting your students from where they are now—up to 100 percent proficiency in twelve years—but your timelines must be based on *equal* increments. And if your schools don't annually achieve those *equal* AYP targets, they're going to be labeled as losers." (Federal lawmakers probably anticipated that if no requirement for *equal* increments had been inserted in the law, state education officials would have opted for eleven years' worth of 2 percent improvements followed by a twelfth-year jump of 78 percent!)

Now, let's assume that a state installs a reasonably defensible set of NCLB tests, and sets a reasonably defensible set of academic achievement standards to define its state's basic, proficient, and advanced levels. Then consider where most American students were performing in 2002–3, and where those students are supposed to be performing in twelve years—that is, every student is to be scoring at proficient or advanced levels on a state's NCLB tests. I'm sure you can recognize there are going to be some hefty improvements required in students' test scores if a state's schools are going to escape a massive number of "failing" labels.

When the federal legislators stipulated that a state's timeline aimed toward 100 percent proficiency in the 2013–14 school year must consist of *equal* increments, those lawmakers were trying to make it impossible for a state's educators to satisfy the law's accountability provisions by establishing tiny improvement expectations during the early years of the law's existence. Many educators are complaining mightily about "unattainable perfection." However, they might want to recognize that NCLB's tough requirements are most likely a response to American educators previously avoiding the ESEA's expectations of AYP via trivial improvement expectations.

How AYP Timelines Will Work

First, a state must decide about its test-based definitions of basic, proficient, and advanced (or definitions of as many additional levels of academic achievement standards as the state decides to employ). Then, until the state installs its chosen NCLB tests (described in the previous chapter) by the 2005–6 school year or earlier, whatever tests were currently being used by the state must be employed to identify the percentages of students who are classified as basic, proficient, or advanced.

Suppose a state currently assesses students in reading and math only in grades three, seven, and ten. Until the additional NCLB-required tests are in place, each school and school district must simply use those existing tests to identify the percentages of a school's children who, based on performance-level expectations that a state had to decide about in early 2003, were classified as either proficient or advanced. To illustrate, if a particular school's test scores indicated that 29 percent of the school's students were classified as proficient, and 7 percent were classified as advanced, then that school would have 36 percent of its students regarded as proficient or above.

Early on, all states had to determine the percentage of students designated as proficient or above in each of the state's schools based on test scores earned during the 2001–2 school year, then rank all the schools from the highest percent (proficient or above) to the lowest percent (proficient or above). Next, counting up from the bottom (that is, starting with the very lowest-percent-proficient school), the proficiency percentage (in math, for example) of the school at the 20th percentile—the school that was 20 percent up from the lowest percent-proficient school—was identified. The percentage of students who were proficient or above in that school became the starting point for a state's twelve-year, equal-increment timeline that would determine whether a given school has attained or failed its annual AYP targets.

The chart on page 28 illustrates a hypothetical AYP timeline for a state whose 20th-percentile school came in with a proficient-or-above level of 40 percent in math. (A separate timeline would be needed for reading/language arts.) According to this timeline, 5 percent increases in the number of proficient-or-above students will be needed each year. If the number of students who were proficient or above in the baseline year (2001–2) had been much lower, then even larger annual increases would be required to satisfy AYP demands. Note also that each of the timeline's twelve increments is one year in length. You'll see in a moment that the *duration* of an AYP timeline's increments turns out to be a pivotal factor.

What I want you to realize from this illustration is that the required percentages of annual increases in the number of students who must be designated as proficient or above on the basis of their test scores is staggering. If defensible tests and defensible performance levels are put in place, then the numbers of students that a state's schools will need to move each year from below proficient to proficient or above are huge. And, of course,

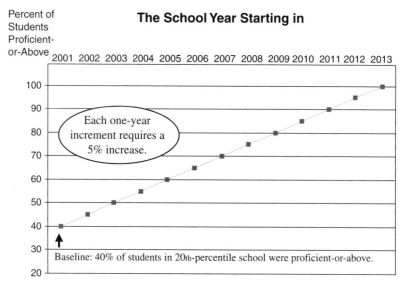

A fictitious twelve-increment state timeline for adequate yearly progress in mathematics, where each of the timeline's increments is one year in length.

given the relentless equal-interval march toward twelve-year complete proficiency, the task gets tougher and tougher each year.

I've talked to officials in several states where their AYP timeline calls for twelve equal, one-year increments. Those officials report that their preliminary projections indicate a school may need to increase its percentage of proficient-or-above students by 5 or 6 percent annually. Is it any surprise that the projections made by those state officials indicate that, within four or five years, almost all of their state's schools will have failed to achieve their state-stipulated AYP targets? And, as a consequence, a majority of those schools will be labeled as failing.

Bending the AYP Timeline

When many of us first reviewed NCLB's requirements for equal increments in a state's timeline, we assumed that states would usually make those increments annual ones, such as the yearly 5 percent incremental increases you saw above. In some states, however, education officials have come up with AYP timelines that they believe will give the state's educators a better chance to avoid AYP-induced failure. Thus, a number of states have crafted more "inventive" AYP timelines, such as the one (from a Midwestern state) presented on the next page.

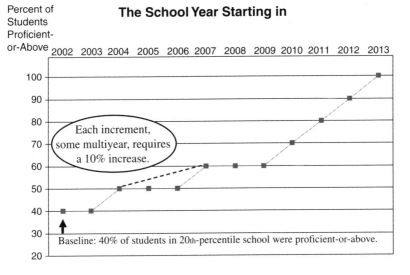

A Midwestern state's six-increment timeline for adequate yearly progress in mathematics, where the timeline's initial increments are two, then three, years in length.

Remember that, according to NCLB, a state can employ one-year, two-year, or three-year intervals in its twelve-year AYP timeline. Because there are serious negative consequences for schools (or districts) that fail to attain their AYP targets for two consecutive years, timelines such as that seen above are clearly intended to reduce the likelihood of AYP failures by spreading out the necessary increases over longer periods of time. Note that there are 10 percent increases in the proportions of proficient-or-better students required during each increment. However, those 10 percent increments start off with a two-year increment, followed by two three-year increments, and then finish with three one-year increments. NCLB stipulates that a state's first AYP increment must take place in not less than two years. Thereafter, the law requires increments in no less than three years. While the architects of these "inventive" AYP timelines have followed the letter of the law, their motivation is all too transparent.

Take a careful look at the way that the multiyear increments are structured in the above figure and I think you'll understand how this dodge-failure strategy is intended to work. By pushing the length of the state's early AYP increments to the absolute legal limits—namely, two years, and then three years—it is hoped that fewer of the state's schools and districts will fail to make their AYP targets in the early years of the law's life. Please consider, for example, the first three-year increment—that is, the increment that begins with the school year starting in 2004 and ends with the school year starting in 2007—marked on the graph with a dotted line. Notice that 50 percent of a school's students must be proficient or above during each of the increment's three years. Yet of course, in the second and third years that was the level required by the *previous* AYP increment! Thus, *in the second two years* of the 2004–7 increment, no increase in the percent of proficient-or-above students is required. It is only at the end of the three-year increment that a 10 percent increase is mandated.

Now, if you look at the one-year increment located between the school years starting in 2009, you'll see that a full 10 percent jump is required each year. Clearly that's a major accomplishment! Why on earth would a state's educational officials call for three *consecutive* increases of 10 percent in their timeline's final three years? The answer is obvious: This set of 10 percent hops at the end was the only way the timeline, as required by law, would ever get to the 100 percent proficient-or-above level by twelve years. By spacing out a 10 percent increment over the two or three legally allowable years at the start, the motivation is clearly to have fewer educators fail, at least initially. However, this sort of timeline strategy surely distorts the law's cornerstone provision of adequate yearly progress. As you can see, in five of this timeline's twelve years, no annual progress at all is required.

Architects of state AYP timelines such as the one seen above sometimes characterize this plan as a "start slow, finish fast" timeline. In my view, such AYP timelines were obviously constructed because of a fervent hope that the expectations embodied in NCLB may, after several years of massive U.S. school failures, be meaningfully reduced by federal lawmakers. Many state-level education officials believe that, after enormous numbers of public schools are labeled failing, NCLB might disappear completely!

IT GETS EVEN STICKIER

Remember when I pointed out earlier in this chapter that AYP was also to be based on the progress of several NCLB-designated subgroups? According to this mandate, sufficient AYP must also be seen in a school for student subgroups reflecting race/ethnicity (that is, white, African American, Hispanic American, Asian American, and Native American students), economically disadvantaged students, students with disabilities, and students with limited English proficiency. Test performances of all these subgroups in a school must be analyzed to see that they, too, are satisfying the state's AYP annual expectations. If there are too few students from any of these subgroups in a particular school (too few students, that is, to provide statistically reliable estimates), that subgroup's performance need not be incorporated in a school's AYP analyses. However, small numbers of these student groups, while insufficient for determining a *school's* AYP status, must be aggregated at the *district* level. Although different states have established different minimum numbers of students in order for a subgroup's performance to be regarded as statistically reliable, many states have set those minimum numbers at between twenty-five and fifty students per subgroup. District-level AYP data, of course, can determine whether a school district is failing.

A Laudable Motive—But with Some Lingering Difficulties

In a very real sense, then, the more students from these legally identified student subgroups that there are in a school—simply on the basis of raw probabilities—the more chances there are for the school to fall short of its AYP targets. (One subgroup's failure to satisfy its AYP targets will mean that the entire school has failed AYP.) The *fewer* NCLB-designated subgroups that are present in a school, the less likelihood there will be of that school's being identified as an AYP-based failing school. While the intentions of the federal lawmakers who crafted NCLB were praiseworthy, by trying to focus educators' attention on the performance levels of these often underserved subgroups, it will turn out that large schools—those having more students and, therefore, a likelihood of more AYP-determining subgroups—are more apt to end up labeled as failing than are low-enrollment schools.

Because the performances of subgroups must be aggregated at the district level, even if there are too few students for statistically reliable subgroup analyses at the school level, a school district could end up having every one of its schools escape a "failing" label individually but, because of the analyses of aggregated district-level subgroup performances, the district itself could be labeled a failure.

One way for state authorities to reduce the number of their state's schools that will be identified as having failed AYP is to require very large minimum numbers of students for AYP-determining subgroup analyses. For instance, if a state's minimum number of students necessary for AYP subgroup analysis was seventy-five, then it's clear that far fewer schools would take an annual tumble on AYP than if that state had set a minimum number of, say, twenty-five students. Parents and educators should be wary of the motives of state officials who establish minimum subgroup numbers much larger than fifty students.

Once more, however, we find "inventive" state education officials trying to elude this AYP-subgroup requirement by employing exotic statistical rationales that end up calling for a school to have remarkably large numbers of students per subgroup before that subgroup's test scores are counted in the school's AYP calculations. If, via statistical machinations, it turns out that unless a school has two hundred or more students in one of NCLB's designated subgroups, it's pretty obvious that few schools need be worried about AYP for that subgroup. There's an old saying, "If you torture statistics long enough, they'll confess to anything." In states where we find that outlandishly large numbers of students are now required for subgroup AYP determination, the torture seems to be working.

As was seen with the establishment of inventive state AYP timelines, requiring very large minimum numbers for including a subgroup's performance in AYP measurements is an obvious attempt to reduce the number of failing schools. After all, if a school need not count a designated subgroup in its AYP calculations because there are too few students in that subgroup, then the school is less apt to flop in attaining its AYP targets. Unfortunately, such tactics will usually end up masking insufficient growth on the part of those students who most need educators' attention.

ANOTHER FAILURE-AVOIDANCE TACTIC

There's yet another statistical wrinkle state officials have recently relied on to make sure that too many schools don't fail AYP, and it is based on a concept familiar to most of us. If you ever watch the results of public opinion polls on television, you'll often see (usually in smaller print at the bottom of the screen) a plus-or-minus estimate—for example, plus or minus 3 percent. The size of this interval can help viewers determine how accurate a given poll's estimates are. For instance, if two candidates are vying for state political office, and a poll is reported showing a 10 percent gap between them, then a plus-or-minus 2 percent sampling error would indicate that the poll's reported gap is much more accurate than would be the case if the poll had a plus-or-minus sampling error of 8 percent. These plus-or-minus sampling errors are useful, because they help us recognize the accuracy/inaccuracy of a sample's findings. The smaller the sampling error the better.

Technically, those plus-or-minus error estimates are referred to as *confidence intervals*. A confidence interval is a statistically sound procedure for determining the degree to which a *sample* is an accurate representation of a *population*. Thus, for instance, when pollsters draw a careful sample of registered voters from the entire population of a state's registered voters, then ask them about their preferences for candidates, the calculation of a confidence interval allows people to tell whether the sample's preferences represent an accurate estimate of the population's preferences. Confidence intervals are good things.

However, in many states we now find education officials relying on confidence intervals simply to reduce the number of schools that fail AYP. The approach is premised on the reasonable notion that any educational test is not perfectly accurate, so there ought to be a mechanism employed to take this inaccuracy into account. That's true, of course, but there are other ways of identifying a test's inaccuracy than through the use of confidence intervals. At bottom, state officials' rationale for using confidence intervals is wrongheaded.

Here's the way that confidence intervals are being used today. State authorities calculate a confidence interval, sometimes 95 percent and sometimes 99 percent, that is used to estimate how *inaccurate* a given school's proportion of proficient-or-above students might be. For instance, a 95 percent confidence interval might be plus or minus 20 percent, which means that if a given school's actual proportion of proficient-or-above students in reading was, say, 18 percent, while the state's required proportion of proficient-or-above students for that year was 35 percent, it would appear that the school would have failed its AYP target. But that's not what happens. Instead, the state's 20 percent confidence interval comes racing to the rescue. Here's how.

The state simply tacks on its plus-or-minus 20 percent confidence interval to that year's already set proficient-or-above proportion of 35 percent, so that a school actually has to fall below the stipulated 35 percent *minus* the 20 percent confidence interval—that is, below 15 percent. So our would-be failing school whose 18 percent proportion of proficient-or-better students looked so weak is actually excused from the failure list because of a "statistical safeguard." It is interesting, of course, that the 20 percent inaccuracy estimate is never *added* to what the state requires for a given year's AYP target. Moreover, the higher the confidence interval, the wider that interval becomes. This means that a 99 percent confidence interval is wider than a 95 percent confidence interval. The wider the confidence interval, the more would-be failing schools there are that will be rescued. Thus, if your state is employing a 99 percent confidence interval to help determine its schools' AYP status, you can be almost certain that the poor performances of many schools are being statistically camouflaged.

This whole confidence-interval strategy, however, is supposed to revolve around how accurately a *sample* represents a *population*. When only 23 percent of Magruder Middle School's students this year score high enough on the state's NCLB math tests to be considered proficient, then what's that a sample of? The students at Magruder who took the math test aren't a sample of anything; they're the population for that school. The whole "sample-based" reliance on confidence intervals is simply a ploy to minimize school failure. The proponents of confidence intervals might suggest that this year's set of students constitute a sample of all the students who might have attended actually the school, or that this year's Magruder students represent a sample of future or past Magruder students. But that's specious reasoning. The use of confidence intervals to reduce school failures is nothing more than a statistical sham. Be wary if your state is using this approach, especially if officials have installed 99 percent intervals.

EXPECTATIONS, ESCAPE, AND UNDERSTANDING

All right, you now probably know more about adequate yearly progress than you ever wanted to. But summing up, AYP will surely be the fulcrum for most schools' NCLB success or failure. You obviously need to understand how AYP works.

When this most recent version of 1965's ESEA (that is, NCLB) was devised, its architects established some altogether unrealistic expectations for the nation's educators. We can understand why federal lawmakers, distressed because of the trivializing of previous AYP goals, imposed what—over a twelve-year span—are absurdly ambitious AYP aspirations. A goal of 100 percent proficiency in twelve years may make for politically appealing rhetoric, but it doesn't make such a goal attainable.

So when a state's education officials attempt to evade AYP requirements with a medley of escapist tactics, we can certainly understand why.[3] No one wants to be regarded as a failure. However, if dodge-the-law gimmicks are concealing certain schools that really do need to be placed on an improvement cycle, then such gimmicks are likely to deprive the children in those schools from improved instruction.

All Americans, and certainly parents and teachers, want our schools to improve over time. In NCLB, AYP is the way that such improvement is supposed to be displayed.

3

Report Cards And Sanctions

Anyone who's ever gone to school, at least in the United States, has surely received a great many report cards. Today's student report cards are substantially different from the ones I received when I attended Sunnyside Grade School and Washington High School in the Portland, Oregon, public schools. Back then, it was pretty clear that an *F* stood for failing performance and an *A* represented exceptional work. But that was a simpler time.

These days a child's report card often seems to be so complex that it requires decryption software to unravel its mysteries. A medley of skills and knowledge are often listed, each of them accompanied by a numerical "grade" based on some sort of altogether unfathomable evaluative scheme. Sometimes these evaluations even incorporate decimals, so parents are led to believe that such decimal-laden numbers positively reek of precision. Exotic and "decimaled" or not, however, all of these report cards focus on how well an individual student is performing in school. Now, NCLB has introduced a whole new variety of required report cards that will soon overlay the land. This new species of report cards is not intended to grade students but, rather, to grade educators or, more plainly, to grade schools.

SCHOOL-FOCUSED REPORT CARDS

Federal law now requires that all states, and all school districts, must provide parents and the public with annual report cards focused directly on the quality of education provided by each of its public schools. For those schools and districts that receive ESEA Title I funds—and about 95 percent of school districts currently receive this funding—there are serious sanctions linked to these report cards. Thus, the school-focused report cards to be issued by both the state and all its school districts will surely receive considerable attention from those who receive them. Moreover, the teachers and administrators in every school will, you can be certain, pay plenty of attention to what's on those report cards.

State-Level Reporting

State report cards about school quality are, by law, to be provided to parents and to the public annually in a concise, yet understandable form. These report cards must also be widely disseminated by the state and its school districts. Several pages in NCLB spell out precisely what these state-level report cards must include. However, the most important requirement is that the state report card must supply information about the proportion of the state's students who have been classified at each of the state's proficiency levels. For example, a state's report card must identify the percent of the state's students who scored at the *proficient* level on the state's NCLB tests, as well as the percent of students classified as *basic, advanced,* or on any other performance levels used in that state. These statewide proportions are to be provided in the aggregate (that is, for all of the state's students), and also in disaggregated fashion so that the proportions of students classified in each of the state's proficiency levels can be seen according to "race, ethnicity, gender, disability status, migrant status, English proficiency, and status as economically disadvantaged." (Notice that gender and migrant status are to be reported in these state-level report cards, but are not used in the calculation of AYP.)

The state report card is also required to compare the actual achievement levels of these students (both the entire student population and the subgroups cited above) with the required minimum improvement percentages of proficient-or-above students that are designated in the state's AYP timeline. Such comparisons, of course, will provide a measure of whether the state's school system (as a whole) is successful in its efforts to have more students classified as proficient-or-above on the state's NCLB tests. Those comparisons will also make it possible to see if a state's schools, overall, are making satisfactory progress according to the total state AYP timeline, both for all students as well as for the designated subgroups.

The state report cards are, in addition, supposed to provide information about *which* of the state's school districts are making AYP. Also to be identified are the number of schools in the state that have not reached their state-determined AYP goals. The names of those "failing" schools, not surprisingly, are also to be given in the state NCLB-required report cards. Of course, the naming of schools that fail AYP transforms the NCLB-based school evaluation game into one that is decidedly "up close and personal." Although there are a number of other required and optional elements that must go into a state's annual report card, I'm sure you can see the thrust of these now-required reports. NCLB intends that states, if they are going to receive the ESEA's Title I dollars, let a state's stakeholders know whether those federal dollars appear to be improving that state's education program.

District-Level Reporting

A state's school *districts* also need to prepare and distribute an annual *district-level* report card to parents and to the public at large. Though they contain the same kind of information now required for state-level report cards, the district report cards are to be more focused on the quality of a given district's schools. For example, the district report cards must indicate the number and percentage of the district's schools not attaining their AYP targets. District-level report cards must also show how the district's students performed on the statewide academic assessments, compared to the performance of the state's students as a whole on those assessments.

If a school has been identified as needing improvement because insufficient numbers of its students—based on state tests—were classified as proficient or better, then this school must be singled out (that is, identified as an AYP-failing school). Moreover, its students' performances on the statewide academic assessments must be compared with the performances of the state's students as a whole.

There may be additional information included in the annual district-level report cards, but the thrust of these reports is quite clear. NCLB calls for districts to supply the public, and especially parents of school-age children, with an annual indication of *how well the district's instructional staff is doing its job*. It will be these district-level report cards that transmit the message to parents that their children are or are not attending a failing school. Teachers, of course, will typically already have learned that theirs is a failing school.

I'll soon supply a brief description of the penalties to be doled out to schools (or districts) that are receiving Title I funds but don't attain their annual AYP targets. First, however, I need to acquaint you with a clever little wrinkle that NCLB incorporates into this scheme regarding which students need to take a state's annual academic assessments.

TESTING AT LEAST 95 PERCENT
OF ENROLLED STUDENTS

The percentages of students not taking the state tests (both for all students and for the AYP subgroups) must be cited in the state and district report cards. NCLB requires that 95 percent of eligible students—that is, those who are enrolled in a school or district—must take the state's NCLB assessments. Let me explain how this seemingly innocent requirement found its way into the law.

In the past, when no 95 percent minimum of test takers was in place for schools receiving the ESEA Title I funds, there were instances in which educators in a given school arranged, on the day of the state test, for the school's lowest-ability students to somehow be unavailable for testing. A special "field trip," for instance, might have been arranged for students who historically had performed poorly on important achievement tests. Clearly, such contrivances were intended to result in higher test scores for the schools involved. However, these sorts of tricks also provided a misleading, and usually deceitful, picture of the entire student body's actual performance.

Thus, as you saw when I described how NCLB's congressional lawmakers require equal-sized AYP increments in students' performances (so as to preclude education officials' setting trivial improvement goals), we now see how those lawmakers attempted to plug another loophole. Because both state and district report cards must indicate the percentage of students not tested, parents of school-age children will now be able to see whether in their children's schools—and also in the school district as a whole—a sufficient percentage of students have been assessed with the state's annual NCLB tests. Because a failure to test at least 95 percent of the eligible students automatically tosses a school into the failed AYP category, this is clearly an important requirement for local educators to satisfy.

AND NOW COME SANCTIONS

All schools, whether they receive Title I funds or not, are to be identified if they fail to satisfy their AYP targets. However, NCLB calls for sanctions to be imposed on those districts or schools that receive the ESEA Title I funds yet whose state-set AYP targets have not been met. If a school gets no Title I dollars, there are no subsequent sanctions for that school. And yet, because about two-thirds of the nation's schools actually do receive Title I funds, a huge number of schools are apt to be sent scurrying down a sanction-laden trail.

In this section I will first describe the formal federally prescribed labels that are to be stamped on the schools that don't perform satisfactorily in the annual AYP rodeo. I'll then briefly indicate what sorts of sanctions for Title I schools accompany those labels.

School Labels and Sanctions

Schools that fail to make AYP for two consecutive years are designated as schools *in need of improvement.* These schools are to develop a "scientifically" based improvement plan. The parents of children in such schools may transfer their child to another public school in the district—one that has not failed AYP—and the district's Title I funds must pay for the transportation of those students to another public school.

Incidentally, even if all the schools in a district have failed AYP and as such are not eligible for the use of within-district student transfers, this does not mean that parents can transfer their children to successful schools in other districts. We have already seen a number of attempts by administrators in high-failure districts to get officials in adjacent districts to voluntarily accept transfers from the high-failure district. So far I've encountered no instance in which such between-district transfers have been accepted by officials in those low-failure districts.

If a school fails to make AYP for three consecutive years, its students are still eligible for public school choice, but those students can also receive a range of supplementary services including after-school tutoring (again, paid for by the district's Title I funds).

Schools that fail to make AYP for four consecutive years are designated as being *in corrective action*. Such schools must then implement an improvement plan that includes such options as developing a new curriculum or replacing certain of the school's staff members.

Schools that have not satisfied their AYP targets for five consecutive years are placed in a *restructuring* category. These schools may be taken over by the state, operated by a private management firm, or converted into charter schools.

Once a school gets placed on this "needs-improvement, corrective-action, restructuring" cycle, that school is going to be regarded by the world at large, and especially by parents who have children in the school, as a failing school. In later chapters I will discuss how to tell whether such "failing" labels are being accurately affixed.

Before turning to what happens when districts stumble on their AYP targets, I need to say just a few words about NCLB's insistence on the use of scientifically proven improvement strategies. Insofar as this NCLB requirement reflects a desire to see educators attempt to improve their schools with procedures and materials that have been carefully evaluated—as opposed to having been dreamed up over the weekend—the advocacy of scientifically researched improvement tactics makes lots of sense.

Of course, I've been working in the field of educational research for over four decades, and I've rarely seen any sort of instructional intervention that has been scientifically *proven* to work. Let's face it, education is a complex arena embracing all sorts of potent variables such as a teacher's personality, a student's prior experiences, and the support of a child's family. Such variables can decisively affect how well a particular improvement-focused strategy will work. So let's be honest about whether there are many scientifically proven procedures and materials sitting on the shelf, ready for instant installation. That's just not so.

District Labels and Sanctions

Districts must also make AYP or they, too, are placed on a must-improve sequence. A district that fails to make AYP for two consecutive years is labeled as *needing improvement*. Such a district must develop an improvement plan and spend at least 10 percent of its Title I funds on the professional development of its staff.

If a district fails AYP for four consecutive years, then the state must take one of several—quite severe—corrective actions regarding that district. For example, the state can (1) replace district personnel deemed to be responsible for the district's failure; (2) authorize students to transfer to schools in another, higher-performing district if that district agrees to accept such transfers; or (3) shut down the district altogether. There are other equally harsh options at the state's disposal, and state officials are required to implement at least one of these legally specified improvement procedures.

I have suggested earlier that a school entering an improvement cycle because it flopped on AYP will often be regarded as a failing school. That same perception will surely arise regarding school districts that fail to make their district-level AYP targets. Interestingly, however, it will be far easier for districts to be regarded as failing under the provisions of NCLB.

Recall from the previous chapter that not only a school's total school population, but also its NCLB-designated subgroups (for example, those based on race or poverty), had to make AYP each year. But, as you have seen, if there are not enough members of one of these legally designated subgroups in a school to provide a statistically reliable estimate of those students' test-based performance levels, then such a group is not to be involved in determining whether the school satisfied its AYP targets. For instance, if in a school there were only seven Native American students, and state officials had previously determined that any subgroups with fewer than thirty students should not be analyzed (because of statistical unreliability) for AYP purposes, then that school would not be held legally accountable for promoting AYP for its Native American students.

However, because a school district must aggregate (from all of its schools) the performances of students from the various NCLB-designated subgroups, a school district will almost certainly have more opportunities (on mere probability grounds alone) to fail to meet its AYP targets than will the district's individual schools. To illustrate, suppose a particular state's "minimum AYP subgroup" number is twenty-five students, and there were seven Native American students in each of a district's four elementary schools. None of the elementary schools would need to demonstrate AYP for their Native American students. The district, however, with its twenty-eight Native American students, would need to do so.

FEDERAL INTENT

Any astute literature professor will tell you that, after one has read a poem or novel, it is almost impossible to identify with certainty what the author was attempting to accomplish. It is almost as risky to try figuring out what the true intent was of the congressional lawmakers who crafted NCLB. However, when you add together the three major components of the law that I've described thus far, I think I can make a pretty decent guess about legislative intent. The key points of NCLB specify that states must

- Administer state-approved but *standardized* achievement tests to *at least 95 percent* of enrolled students in specified grade levels.
- Establish *stringent, equal-increment* AYP targets for all students as well as for designated student subgroups.
- Make sure that state and district *report cards*, focused on an NCLB-specified set of evaluative dimensions, are widely disseminated so that schools and districts receiving Title I funds, but failing their AYP targets, must enter into an improvement cycle.

To me, the foregoing requirements clearly indicate that NCLB's federal lawmakers wanted educational improvements to take place across the nation but simply did not trust public school educators to attain those improvements without heavy-handed help. Accordingly, NCLB's architects set up a series of evidence-gathering requirements, some of which are remarkably challenging, and then created rules to make sure the public—and especially parents of kids in school—would have ample opportunities to consider such evidence.

The legislative strategy, or so it seems, was to create evidence-gathering mechanisms by which to evaluate school quality, then lay the resulting evidence at the feet of the educators and parents who could (and should) make a difference in the way a state's schools are operated.

Let me lay my bias on the table early, so as not to be accused of blind-siding later on. Given *some* education officials' previously displayed skill in subverting the evaluative requirements of federal reform-focused legislation, I can see why there are so many unbending procedural constraints in NCLB. If NCLB is properly implemented, however, I believe it can lead to a far better education for our nation's children.

Yet that innocent little *if* makes all the difference. Because NCLB is so heavily dependent on the test performances of students, it is imperative that the right tests be employed to implement the law. With the right tests (that is, suitable state "academic achievement assessments"), NCLB can accomplish great good. With the wrong kinds of tests, this potentially beneficial law will end up harming children—and harming them seriously.

If you have a child or a grandchild in school, read on. If you teach in a public school or are simply concerned about the state of the education system in our society today, read on. You'll see that the entire NCLB accountability structure, if erected on the basis of the wrong kinds of state tests, will collapse like a sand castle trying to do a battle with a high tide. *Whether NCLB wins or loses depends primarily on the tests that are used to implement this significant federal law.* Educational tests are, indeed, the heart of the matter. And that's what the next part of this book is about.

PART II

Educational Tests:
The Heart of the Matter

4

Some Nuts and Bolts
of Educational Testing

Educational test results, as I noted earlier, are playing an ever more important role in determining the quality of U.S. public schools. This is the chief reason that anyone seeking to understand the pressures on public schools today needs to know at least a few basic things about how educational tests work. In this chapter, I'll be introducing some nuts-and-bolts concepts in educational testing that play a significant role in the debate surrounding NCLB reforms.

THE PURPOSE OF EDUCATIONAL TESTING: INFERENCE MAKING

The first of these concepts to consider is the purpose of educational testing. The reason that educators test children is to make an *inference* about the knowledge or skills that a child possesses. Here's how such test-based inferences work.

Test-Based Inferences

Although teachers can readily see how tall a child is, they can't look at that child and tell how much the child knows about geography or how well the child can read. A student's skills and knowledge are not observable. Teachers thus give tests in order to make an *inference*—that is, an interpretation—about the child's unseen skills and knowledge. For instance, when Kris takes a twenty-item spelling test and answers all twenty items correctly, the inference the teacher typically makes is that Kris is a pretty good speller. On the other hand, if Sean spells only five of the test's twenty spelling words correctly, the teacher usually infers that Sean's spelling skills are weak and in need of improvement.

Though these assessments are sometimes referred to as "valid tests," it isn't the test that's valid or invalid. Instead, it's the inference, made from the student's test performance, that's either valid or invalid. There is no such thing as a valid, every-time-a-bulls'-eye educational test. Educational tests, when taken by students, produce scores, and human beings then make inferences about what those scores mean. But human beings, as we know all too well from experience, have been known to make mistakes! If you understand that it is someone's interpretive judgment about what a test performance signifies—and not the test itself—that's either valid or invalid, you'll realize people's judgments may or may not be accurate.

The first relevant concept, then, is that the fundamental purpose of educational assessment is to permit teachers (or parents) to arrive at valid (that is, accurate) inferences about students' knowledge or skills. Those inferences are based on the way that students have performed on educational tests. And the resulting inferences are then used by teachers to make instructional decisions about their students.

Test-Based Inferences and Classroom Instruction

The way that classroom teaching is conducted in most settings is determined by a number of factors. First, decisions are made about the knowledge and skills that students should master. Educators have historically used the term *curriculum* to describe such knowledge and skills. These days, however, an equally popular descriptor for the knowledge and skills students are supposed to learn is *content standards*. In order for us to be suitably fashionable, let's use that label from here on in. I'll dig more deeply into the nature of content standards later, in chapter 6.

Next, a teacher plans and carries out lessons that the teacher hopes will help students master the content standards that have been selected. This is what happens in the classroom and it can be described as *teaching* (or, if you prefer, as *instruction*). Typically, then, after the instruction has been concluded, students are assessed to see how well they have mastered the knowledge and skills that were promoted during instruction. At that point, teachers ordinarily use students' test results to make an inference about the degree to which students have actually mastered the knowledge and skills represented by the content standards. That test-based inference is then used by teachers to make instructional decisions, such as whether to give students additional instruction or to instead move on to a new topic.

This process can be represented graphically where you can see that the teacher starts with the curriculum (that is, content standards), provides instruction, assesses students after instruction is over, then draws test-based inferences about students' achievements. These inferences typically allow the teacher to decide whether the previously provided instruction has been effective or if those instructional activities need to be altered. In other words, these test-based inferences allow teachers to determine whether their students have learned what they were supposed to learn.

Test-based inferences usually lead the teacher to conclude that (1) the instruction does/doesn't need to be altered, or (2) the content standards originally selected do/don't need to be altered. For instance, a test-based

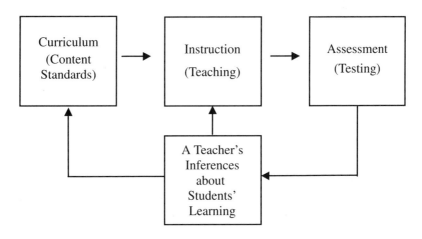

The way that test-based inferences function in a typical classroom.

inference might indicate that the teacher's instruction fell flat on its face. Clearly, the teacher needs to make serious modifications in such ineffective instructional activities. But it's also possible that a test-based inference suggests that students are finding the teacher's content standards insufficiently challenging. Thus, the teacher may need to augment the originally selected content standards. As you can see in the figure on page 51, the teacher's test-based inferences typically feed back into decisions about curriculum, instruction, or (sometimes) both.

What you need to recognize is that educational tests provide evidence used to make inferences. If the test is a good one and the inference maker is sensible, then the resulting inference will be valid. But tests by themselves do not make inferences—people do—and the entire instructional process commences with the content standards teachers have been told to promote. If inappropriate content standards are chosen (for example, curricular aims that are trifling or those that are far too difficult for the students), then it's certain that educators' instructional efforts won't lead to what they're supposed to—namely, well-educated boys and girls.

Two Types of Test-Based Inferences

The second assessment concept you need to know deals with the two types of test-based inferences that educators make regarding their students. Those inferences, and the way that students' performances are reported to parents, must either be *relative* or *absolute*. These days, with what seems like ever-increasing frequency, parents are receiving test-based reports about their children's in-school academic achievements. It's important, therefore, to look at how these reports ought to be interpreted.

Relative Score Reports

A *relative score report* indicates how a student's performance compares to that of other students. For instance, when the parents of a fourth-grade student learn that she scored at the 67th *percentile* in mathematics on a standardized achievement test, this means she outperformed 67 percent of the fourth graders who were included in the test's *norm group*. A norm group is a representative sample of students who completed a standardized test soon after it was developed. A standardized test, by the way, is simply a test that must be administered and scored in a standard, predetermined manner.

Because traditional standardized tests invariably use norm-group comparisons to interpret a given student's scores, many educators describe such tests as "norm-referenced." That's because, to infer what a child's score actually means, educators must "reference" that child's score back to the scores made by the test's norm group.

Learning how a child stacks up against other children, of course, can be quite useful; relative score reports, as I just pointed out, can be genuinely helpful to parents and to teachers. If Tom's parents learn that his scores on a nationally standardized achievement test indicate he is performing at the 91st percentile in language arts (that's good!), but at the 23rd percentile in mathematics (that's not so good!), then Tom's parents could talk to the teachers at his school to make sure those teachers are attending to his less-than-lofty mathematics skills. Tom's teachers can, clearly, also profit from such relative score reports.

Absolute Score Reports

Relative score reports, as you can see, are always based on one student's test performance compared to the performances of other students. *Absolute score reports*, on the other hand, focus on what it is that the child can or can't do. For example, if the content standard being assessed is a student's skill in interpreting scientific tables and graphs, an absolute score report would indicate how well the child could perform that particular interpretive skill. The report might say something such as the student has mastered this skill at a "proficient," or perhaps at an "advanced," level.

Educational tests built chiefly to provide absolute interpretations are sometimes referred to by educators as "criterion-referenced" because, when interpreting scores, educators "reference" the student's performance back to a clearly described criterion behavior such as a well-defined skill or body of knowledge.

For purposes of instructional planning, teachers need an idea of what it is that students actually can or can't do. Absolute score reporting schemes are far more useful—instructionally—to both teachers and parents. That's because such reports indicate more clearly what it is the child already knows or, in contrast, what the child needs to work on. Relative scores fail to provide such clarity, for they offer only a comparative picture of the child's attainments. Although such comparative interpretations can be helpful to both teachers and parents, the instructional usefulness of such interpretations is quite limited. Typically, absolute score reports are supplied either as "percent-of-mastery" reports or "performance labels" such as *basic, proficient*, or *advanced*. Those performance labels, however, are based on someone's decision about what percent of mastery is necessary for students to display in order to be regarded as, for example, *advanced*.

To illustrate the difference in the way that parents might be given a relative score report versus an absolute score report, think about a nationally standardized spelling test based on a student's ability to correctly spell five hundred words that—at each grade level—have been identified by the test's publisher as "important but hard to spell words." After students have taken the test, a relative score report to Maria's parents might indicate that "Maria's test score was equivalent to a 71st percentile based on the performances of the test's national norm group." What that report means, of course, is that Maria scored better on the spelling test than 71 percent of the students in the norm group who had previously completed that test. Percentiles are, by far, the most commonly used form of relative score reports. That's because percentiles are intuitively understandable to most people.

In contrast, again using the same standardized spelling test based on the five hundred tough spelling words chosen at each grade, an absolute score report to Miguel's parents might read something along these lines: "Your son's test performance indicates that he has mastered 92 percent of the five hundred spelling words designated for his grade level." So, while relative "percentile" score reports deal with how a child's test performance compares to those of other children, an absolute "percent-correct" score report tries to describe what it is that a student can or can't do with respect to whatever the test is supposed to be measuring. There is, as you can see, a meaningful difference between a relative test score's percentile reports and an absolute test score's percent-of-mastery or performance-label reports. Many parents don't understand this key distinction between relative and absolute score reporting. As a consequence, confusion sometimes follows.

The Imprecision of Educational Testing

This brings us to a third significant concept, namely, the precision of educational measurement or more accurately the *imprecision* of such measurement. This is a simple but important point—namely, that educational testing is far less precise than most parents (and numerous educators) think it is.

Many parents believe that when they receive a score report about their child's test performance—whether the report is based on a teacher's classroom quiz or is derived from a state or nationally standardized test—that score is really quite accurate. That's often just not so. The fact that a test yields a numerical score does not signify that the score provides a truly precise picture of a student's achievements. On any given day, a child's test performance can yield a very misleading inference about that child's actual abilities.

Many factors can make a test score inaccurate. For example, there might be ambiguous items in the test itself; the child may not be feeling well on the day the test was taken; the child may have eaten too little, or too much, before the test; or the child may also have been excessively anxious about the test. That's especially true for very important tests. Then, too, on any given day a student may simply get lucky and guess correctly most of the time or, in contrast, may have a bad-luck day and come up with many incorrectly guessed answers. Sometimes students—especially teenagers—don't take tests as seriously as educators hope, so the students don't try to do their best. In short, there are numerous factors that can reduce the accuracy of students' test scores.

Measurement experts know this very well. They've even created a formula to help them estimate how imprecise a given test score is likely to be. It's called the "standard error of measurement." Note that the name of the formula accurately conveys the idea that measurement errors are *standard*, not exceptional. This is why it is always more defensible to base an inference regarding a child's status on several different assessments rather than on one single test.

The commonly held idea that educational tests are superaccurate really needs to be squashed. Educational tests do provide useful information for both teachers and parents, but that information should be regarded as imperfect, and far from flawlessly accurate. A test score should be seen only as a rough *approximation* of a student's actual achievement level.

Varieties of Educational Tests

The last concept about educational tests I want to stress relates to the types of educational tests that are currently in use. Depending on how people categorize such tests, either those constructed by a classroom teacher or those developed by a commercial test firm, the key to

understanding a test is to focus on what a child must do when responding
to a given test.

Three Types of Items

First off, a student can be asked in a test item to select a correct response
from two or more choices. Measurement specialists call these, not surprisingly, *selected-response* items. The most common examples of these sorts of
items are multiple-choice items and true/false items. One substantial
advantage of selected-response items is that they're easy to score, both for
teachers and for computer-based scoring machines.

Second, the student might be asked to supply a short answer to a
question. For example, the item may require a student to provide a sentence
or, possibly, just a word or phrase. The advantage of short-answer items is
that they require the student to generate a correct answer from scratch,
not merely recognize a correct answer from a group of already presented
alternatives (as is the case with all selected-response items). A student
who can generate a correct answer typically possesses the skill or knowledge being assessed at a deeper level than a student who can only identify
a correct answer from a test item's alternatives. Short-answer items, of
course, require more time to score than do selected-response items.

Finally, we come to performance tasks such as those seen when a
statewide testing program calls for students to write an original essay, or
when an English teacher requires a student to present an impromptu
speech to the rest of the class. Performance tasks, of course, more closely
resemble what is required of students in the real world. But performance
tasks are also more difficult—and, because scoring of such items takes
time, much more costly—to score. Performance tasks can vary dramatically in what they ask students to do. From a measurement point of
view, however, there's very little difference among the performance tasks
used to determine whether a student can write a persuasive essay, fill out
a job application form, or repair a malfunctioning carburetor in an auto-
motive class.

When students tackle a performance task such as observing a scientific
experiment and then writing up the experiment's results, the students'
responses are typically scored using what is called a *rubric*. *Rubric* is simply
a highbrow name for a scoring guide.

Properly constructed rubrics can be very helpful to teachers and to their
students. That's because a properly constructed rubric can set out, in clear

language, just what's important for students to include in a satisfactory response to performance tasks measuring a particular skill. Teachers can target their instruction accurately at what's most important for students to learn. Parents, too, can use a properly constructed rubric to help them if they want to supply some at-home support for their children. However, many of the rubrics now found in our schools are of little, if any, instructional value.

These instructionally dysfunctional rubrics are often far too general. Or perhaps they are focused on students' responses to a particular performance task rather than on the students' mastery of the skill that's represented by the task. What parents need to know is that although rubrics *can* be instructionally useful, some rubrics definitely are not. Parents should not be cowed merely because a teacher announces that students' responses are being "scored by a rubric." Everything depends on the caliber of the rubric. In any event, in some states that, a few years ago, began to use statewide achievement tests containing a great many performance tasks, state officials have, unfortunately, now been forced to eliminate most of those kinds of tasks. Performance tasks, at least a swarm of them, were far too expensive to score.

Many educational tests contain all three sorts of items—that is, selected-response items, short-answer items, and performance-task items. But some tests are made up of only one kind of item. Teachers, for example, often use classroom quizzes or exams containing only true/false items or, perhaps, only short-answer items. And some standardized achievement tests are made up of only multiple-choice items. But the exclusive use of selected-response items on standardized tests is becoming rather rare these days—in part because of widespread criticisms about any test that only asks children to choose among already presented answer choices.

So it's apparent that today's teachers typically use a variety of classroom assessments to get a fix on their students' progress. That's less so with statewide tests, chiefly because of the costs involved. Nevertheless, most statewide tests these days ask students to at least tackle some short-answer items and some performance tasks. The most commonly used performance tasks are those requiring students to compose an original essay. NCLB-required tests that I've seen in many states tend to contain at least a modest number of performance-task items.

APTITUDE VERSUS ACHIEVEMENT TESTS

There's one final distinction between types of educational tests that you need to know about—namely, the difference between *achievement* tests and *aptitude* tests. Many people become confused these days by the incredible jumble of letters currently used to describe educational tests. That confusion is certainly understandable, but it's less likely to occur if you know the fundamental difference between an aptitude test and an achievement test.

Achievement tests are supposed to measure the skills and knowledge a student possesses. So, for example, when the Iowa Tests of Basic Skills are given to elementary school children, the intention underlying that testing is, at least in a general way, to get a fix on what knowledge or skills the children possess. Other examples of such achievement tests are the Stanford Achievement Tests and the California Achievement Tests.

Aptitude tests, on the other hand, are supposed to predict how well a student will perform in a subsequent academic setting. That's, for example, what the ACT and the SAT, America's two most dominant college admission exams, are intended to do. At bottom, the chief mission of both the ACT and the SAT is to predict how well a high school student will perform later on in college. In a very real way, aptitude tests are intended to function somewhat like group intelligence tests.

Because there are many factors that contribute to a child's success in college, increasing criticism has been leveled against aptitude-focused college admission tests. In fact, research shows that about 75 percent of a student's success in college is unrelated to that student's score on the ACT or SAT. It is for such reasons that some colleges have threatened to stop using the ACT or SAT as admission tests. Happily, the era of a single test's serving as a sole college admissions criterion seems to be ending. Today's colleges and universities are definitely attempting to use multiple sources of information when admitting students.

Frankly, if you were to review many actual items from an aptitude test, you might think they came from an achievement test—and vice versa. But the two types of tests are constructed with different measurement missions in mind.

Most parents, understandably, want their children to score high enough on college admissions tests so that those children will have an opportunity to get into a good college or university. Such parents' attention, therefore, should be directed to learning more about aptitude tests such as the ACT or SAT. Increasingly, however, state officials are linking high school graduation and grade-to-grade promotions to students' scores on whatever achievement tests are used in that state, and parents in such states need to learn more about these high-stakes achievement tests. The NCLB-required tests that must be administered once in grades ten through twelve, for example, yield scores that colleges can readily incorporate into their admission models. The more that parents understand about aptitude and achievement tests, and the differing purposes of those two types of tests, the more likely it is that parents will be able to make solid decisions about helping their children in relation to such tests.

Having described the distinctions among three kinds of items that are used in educational tests (namely, selected-response, short-answer, and performance-task items) and highlighted the difference between aptitude and achievement tests, there's one more small, but pivotal, point I need to make regarding educational tests—or, more specifically, about their quality.

Educational tests definitely differ in their purpose, but they also differ in their quality. Parents need to recognize that whether educational tests have been created by commercial test development companies or by classroom teachers, some tests will be better than others. Do not assume, automatically, that all educational tests are winners. Unfortunately, some aren't.

Let's consider, first, commercially developed tests—tests typically accompanied by all sorts of technical information. Is it automatically the case that a commercially generated test is a good one? Of course not. There are increasing demands on commercial test development firms to create—and to score—many, many tests. This is especially true since the passage of NCLB. Given today's test construction demands on measurement companies' finite capacities, officials from some test development firms candidly confess that a number of their newly developed tests are not as good as they really could be.

In recent years, there have been many news stories about actual items in widely adopted, commercially constructed tests that have turned out to have two right answers or—worse (from the student's perspective)—no right answers at all. And then there have been frequent reports in the media about electronically misscored standardized tests. Mistakes clearly happen, even in well-established assessment firms, and these mistakes are reflected in the test scores issued by these reputable companies.

The problems generated by classroom tests may be even more significant. Only slightly more than a dozen of our nation's states currently require teachers in training to complete a course in educational testing prior to being licensed. The reality is that many of our nation's teachers know relatively little about educational testing. As a consequence, most of the classroom tests those teachers create for their own classrooms turn out to be astonishingly similar to the tests that those same teachers were given—way, way back—when they, themselves, were students in school.

Thus, although many teachers have—since completing their teacher education programs—taken courses or workshops in the construction of classroom tests, many teachers have not. Teachers, of course, try to do a first-rate job of constructing and interpreting their own classroom tests. But sensible parents should be alert to the possibility that the classroom tests being given to their children's teachers sometimes may be less than terrific. Teachers know this quite well.

Because of the increased significance of test scores, particularly in an educational era soon to be dominated by NCLB's accountability requirements, issues related to educational testing have taken on greater urgency. As we've seen, educational tests are used to make performance-based inferences—that is, *interpretations*—about children's unseen skills or knowledge, and students' test performances are reported to both teachers and parents either relatively or absolutely. Educational tests differ in item type, purpose, and quality, and are much less precise than most people think.

In later chapters we'll look at ways to evaluate tests to determine how well they reflect the quality of a student's instruction. But first let's turn to some of the negative consequences of using tests that, in many ways, fail to accurately measure those things they were meant to assess.

5

Measuring Temperature
with a Tablespoon

Pretend that you are a parent of a four-year-old daughter who has been unusually quiet and inactive for the past few hours. You touch her forehead and discover that it seems warm. Clearly, you are concerned. So you head to the kitchen, take a tablespoon from one of the kitchen drawers, then return to your daughter's side so you can use the tablespoon—to take her temperature. I'm sure you recognize that if you tried to measure a child's temperature with a tablespoon instead of a thermometer most folks would think you're rather confused. Unfortunately, in education there's a lot of confused behavior taking place these days, because people are judging the effectiveness of our schools using measurement tools that are absolutely wrong for such a purpose.

TEST SCORES TRUMP

As we've seen, the presence of NCLB is going to make a big difference in the way that most educators operate. Each school is going to be under the gun to show the world that the school's students are making AYP. The law calls for school districts to issue annual report cards informing students' parents how well their own child's school staff is doing. Based on those reports, the pressure on a school's teachers and administrators to make AYP each year will be substantial. And, of course, the dominant determinant of whether a particular school is a winner or a loser on AYP is the performance of the school's students on the state's annually administered NCLB achievement tests.

If students do not score well enough each year on the state's tests for the school to satisfy its annual AYP target of getting a specified percentage of its students to earn proficient-or-above scores, then that school will be regarded as unsuccessful. Such an AYP-failing school is likely to be regarded by parents, citizens in general, and members of a school district's governing board, as a "failing" school. There may be other information included in those district reports about schools, such as attendance levels, tardiness statistics, or students' grades. But the stark reality is that the overridingly important factor for establishing a school's successfulness—according now to federal law—will be students' scores on the state's NCLB tests. And that's why the selection of NCLB tests at the state level is absolutely the most important factor that will render NCLB beneficial or harmful.

If you live in a state where sensible decisions have been made about statewide NCLB tests, then there's a good chance that the "failing" labels plastered on certain of your state's schools will be accurate. If, on the other hand, you live in a state where officials have installed the wrong kinds of NCLB tests, then these labels for your state's schools will be no more accurate than if you used a tablespoon to take a child's temperature.

I'd like you to make a pair of assumptions that will be helpful in understanding how pivotal it is for states to employ the right kinds of NCLB tests. First, I want you to assume that the NCLB tests a state has selected are *instructionally insensitive.* In other words, assume that the state's annual NCLB tests in grades three through eight and at one point in grades ten through twelve are unable to detect even high-quality instruction if it is present. I know this sounds crazy, but be patient for a bit.

Now I want you to make your second assumption—namely, that the reason for a state NCLB test's instructional insensitivity is that the test is actually an indicator of the kinds of students who attend a school rather than how well that school's students have been instructed. In other words, your second assumption is to regard an NCLB-required test as instructionally insensitive because it measures not what students are taught *in* school but what those students brought *to* school.

If a state's NCLB tests were instructionally insensitive, then each year's administration of those tests would obviously fail to identify either (1) schools where teachers were instructing well or (2) schools where teachers were instructing badly. Effective instruction would not be distinguishable from ineffective instruction, at least on the basis of the scores students made on instructionally insensitive tests.

In fact, in the real world, NCLB tests chosen by many states are altogether instructionally insensitive, built using test construction models that are completely inappropriate for evaluating a school's quality. As you've already seen, the annual NCLB-induced pressure on teachers for their school's students to score high enough for AYP purposes will have a big-time impact on classroom instruction. Teachers will, quite understandably, be doing the things in class they think they need to do in order for the required numbers of their students to achieve proficient-or-above scores on the state's NCLB tests.

In this chapter I'll focus on the negative classroom consequences in so many schools as a direct result of trying to evaluate a school's quality by using the wrong educational tests. You'll see, for example, what happens when teachers' test preparation becomes excessive. Most important, perhaps, you'll find out why it is that certain types of educational tests are so ill-suited for the evaluation of schools. Finally, we'll consider whether there's anything that can be done to remedy a situation now almost certain to undermine whatever good intentions were present in NCLB.

HIGH-STAKES TESTS

As you'll soon recognize, concerns about educational testing rise dramatically whenever students' achievement is being assessed by what is often referred to as a *high-stakes* test. But what is a "high-stakes" achievement test?

A high-stakes educational test is one that has serious consequences —either for the students who take the test or for those who prepared students for that test. For example, if a student's score on a basic skills test can lead to the student's failing to be promoted to the next grade, that would clearly be a high-stakes test. And if a student is denied a diploma because of a low score on a graduation exam, then that too is surely a high-stakes test—for the student and for that student's family.

But it's also true that tests become high-stakes tests if the schools in a state or county are *ranked* on the basis of students' test scores. Thus, when local newspapers publish these rankings, implying that schools whose students score well are effective while schools whose students score poorly are ineffective, you can bet that those tests are also of a high-stakes nature. That is, the evaluative impact of such school ranking is significant to the educators whose competence is thought to be reflected by students' test scores. Because, as we've seen, a state's NCLB tests are going to be used to identify schools and districts that have failed to attain their AYP targets, you can bet (with total confidence of winning) that any state's NCLB tests are going to be super-high-stakes assessments.

Let's look at the chief reason high-stakes tests are given to students in the first place. Most thoughtful people recognize that educational accountability typically underlies the use of high-stakes tests. If you look behind any policy establishing a high-stakes educational test, you'll almost always find someone who has serious doubts about the quality of schooling. Educational accountability systems can not only let citizens know about the effectiveness of their schools but can also, if properly devised, help improve instructional quality. As a measure of educational accountability, high-stakes tests can be beneficial—if they are the right kinds of educational tests. But, in most parts of the country today, the wrong kinds of NCLB high-stakes tests are being used to judge schools.

THE HARMFUL CONSEQUENCES
OF EDUCATIONAL MISMEASUREMENT

I believe that the vast majority of our nation's public school teachers are trying their best to do a good job for the students they teach. I was one of those public school teachers, and I've worked with hundreds of teachers during my career. However, an unsoundly implemented NCLB will place teachers in a no-win accountability game, and for some teachers that situation will lead to classroom conduct that harms students.

Because there is currently so much attention being given to students' test scores, in any setting where there's a high-stakes test, educators are being pressured—and sometimes pressured enormously—to raise students' test scores. These pressures typically lead to three harmful consequences.

Curricular Reductionism

First, because of substantial pressures to raise students' scores on high-stakes tests, in many instances we find educators abandoning significant curricular content not measured by their local high-stakes tests. Skills and knowledge that, only a few years ago, were regarded by teachers as imperative for students have been cut simply because such curricular content is not being measured by whatever high-stakes test is used in that setting. Such discarded content is seen to take up "too much time," and it obviously doesn't contribute to better scores on the high-stakes test. As a result, children are being shortchanged regarding curricula. They're not learning the full-range of what they should be learning because a high-stakes test has triggered cuts in important but untested curricular content.

Many parents and teachers are worried about this adverse curricular impact of high-stakes testing. Both privately and publicly, educators themselves express even greater worries about the curricular impact of high-stakes assessments. A sensible teacher will realize that content measured on a high-stakes test should probably be given a bigger instructional bang than content not measured by that test—regardless of the untested content's true significance to children's learning. And, distressingly, that's precisely what happens in many classrooms. Content not assessed on a high-stakes test is content cast aside.

Excessive Test Preparation

A second harmful consequence of inappropriate high-stakes tests is that some test-pressured teachers now devote a staggering amount of time to drilling their students in preparation for an upcoming high-stakes test. I've personally talked to many teachers who say that, in their schools, all forms of instruction—other than outright drilling for a high-stakes test—are prohibited four to six weeks before the high-stakes test is to be given. That's simply bad educational practice! If schools become only skill-and-drill test preparation factories, how can children derive genuine satisfaction from such drudgery?

Be assured that wherever high-stakes tests are installed, "test-prep fever" is almost certain to follow. The question worrying many parents is whether their children are truly being educated or are simply being groomed to perform well on high-stakes tests. In most parts of our nation where significant standardized tests are used—and that's either off-the-shelf tests such as the Metropolitan Achievement Tests or customized state-built high-stakes tests—parents ought to be worried about how much test preparation time their children are being forced to endure.

Growing numbers of educators are also becoming alarmed about the amount of test preparation that's taking place in today's classrooms. One second-grade teacher sadly told me that she must be preoccupied about whether her second graders will perform well enough on state-administered tests. That's right—second graders! As early as the first and second grade, students are being readied for state-required nationally standardized achievement tests such as the Terra Nova and the Iowa Tests of Basic Skills.

Unethical Test Preparation Practices

As just noted, under relentless pressure to boost their students' test scores, some teachers may end up by providing students with item-focused test preparation because they can't figure out what skills and knowledge are supposed to be represented by a high-stakes test. This is regrettable, but understandable, because teachers are being required to take part in a badly conceived accountability enterprise. Students will often be given practice exercises consisting of items very similar to a test's actual items or, in some instances, the actual items themselves. Along with those practice items, teachers typically supply students with their very own correct answer keys.

Later, when students take the actual test for which they have been prepared, those students encounter identical, or nearly identical, items on which they have been practicing. The students immediately recognize that they have been made unwilling conspirators in a teacher-engineered fraud! Moreover, such item-focused test preparation typically increases students' test scores without actually increasing students' mastery of the skills and knowledge being measured by the test.

As a result of such test preparation practices, both teachers and parents get a misleading idea about a student's true abilities. Putting it another way, any score-based inferences about a student's achievements will most likely be invalid. Teachers can't judge the caliber of their own instructional efforts if they rely on invalid test-based inferences.

Taken together, these three negative consequences of using inappropriate high-stakes tests seriously erode the quality of education many of the nation's children are now receiving. Perhaps in your local schools, children are receiving an inferior education simply because of the presence of an inappropriate high-stakes test. And what you must recognize is that the expansion of NCLB-required achievement testing in our nation's public schools is certain to increase the amount of high-stakes testing in those schools. As a result, the potential for test-triggered educational harm is all the more likely.

UNSUITABLE TESTS FOR EVALUATING SCHOOLS

What are these "inappropriate" high-stakes educational tests that I've been sniping at? There are actually two types of tests that won't allow NCLB to work the way its federal originators hoped. Both types of tests are instructionally insensitive. In this chapter I want to consider the traditionally constructed standardized achievement tests that have become almost ubiquitous in our nation's schools. In the next chapter I'll focus on a second variety of instructionally insensitive achievement tests. Let's begin by dealing with the five most widely adopted, nationally standardized achievement tests in use today—namely, the California Achievement Tests, the Comprehensive Tests of Basic Skills (now known as the Terra Nova), the Iowa Tests of Basic Skills, the Metropolitan Achievement Tests, and the Stanford Achievement Tests. All five of these achievement tests have been around for decades. Many of today's adults, when they were in school, took one or more of these nationally standardized achievement tests.

You may be surprised to hear me say that, in fact, all five of these tests are first-rate educational measuring instruments. They do what they are supposed to do, and they do it well. But they were never intended to be used to evaluate schools, and they just can't do that properly. Yet, because most Americans believe that nationally standardized achievement tests are appropriate for evaluating schools, you'll hear very few protests when these tests are used for that purpose. Believe me, not one of these five standardized tests is suitable for evaluating schools, as you'll soon see.

Standardized achievement tests can provide both teachers and parents with an idea of a student's relative performance. As you saw in chapter 4, relative score reports can provide useful information. If a parent or teacher learns that a child, in relationship to other children, is very strong in math but very weak in reading, steps can be taken to strengthen the child's reading performance. In reality, the overriding mission of nationally standardized achievement tests has always been to produce a sufficient *spread of students' scores* so that an individual student's score can be compared with the scores of students in a norm group—that is, a representative sample of previous test takers. As you'll soon discover, it is this unrelenting quest for score spread that turns out to make nationally standardized achievement tests unsuitable for evaluating schools.

Three Strikes and You're Out!

There are *three* reasons that traditionally constructed standardized achievement tests shouldn't be used to evaluate schools. Let's consider each of these important reasons.

Unrecognized Teaching–Testing Mismatches

Even though most people recognize that there's way too much test preparation stimulated by externally imposed standardized tests, there's a related problem with these tests that's not widely recognized. Simply put, the problem is that teachers can't figure out what's going to be assessed by these tests. Because the test development companies that create nationally standardized tests need to make their one-size-must-fit-all achievement tests acceptable to educators in states whose curricular content varies (at least to some extent), there is some marketing payoff in keeping the descriptions of tested content fairly general—that is, not specific enough to be regarded by prospective purchasers as inconsistent with local curricular preferences.

In a carefully controlled study carried out at Michigan State University, researchers reported that as much as 80 percent of the content on a nationally standardized achievement test may not be meaningfully taught in a given school. How fair do you think it is to evaluate a school using a high-stakes test in which only 20 percent of the test's content is even *supposed* to be taught? Teaching–testing mismatches, if they are serious, surely make standardized tests unsuitable for the evaluation of schools.

Clearly, many of today's teachers find themselves in a real dilemma. They're often supposed to raise their students' scores on nationally standardized achievement tests, but those tests don't clarify just what skills and knowledge the tests are supposed to be measuring. As an understandable consequence, we find teachers looking at a test's actual items, then trying to teach their students to perform well on those or similar items.

But such item-focused teaching often fails to help students master the skills and content on which the test was supposedly based. Item-focused teaching will not help students learn what they need to learn.

A Tendency to Eliminate Items Measuring Important Content

A second problem with traditionally constructed standardized achievement tests is that because of their need to produce sufficient score spread the developers of these tests often end up tossing out test items that cover the most important things teachers teach. Sounds bizarre? Here's how it happens.

In order for standardized tests to permit accurate comparisons among students' scores—for instance, between students who scored at the 78th and 79th percentiles, a test's scores must be well spread out. Indeed, as pointed out in chapter 4, these tests are often described as "norm-referenced" because they allow us to compare a particular student's score to the performance of a norm group. For comparative purposes, there must be some low scores, some high scores, and plenty of scores in the middle. In traditional standardized tests, the more spread out that scores are, the better. If the test scores are grouped too closely together the whole comparative mission of these tests collapses. In short, for those who construct traditional standardized achievement tests, score spread is not merely desirable, it is a necessity.

In the relatively brief time that educators have at their disposal for testing a student in a particular subject—and that's usually about an hour or so—test developers need items that will produce a suitable amount of score spread. From a statistical perspective, test items answered correctly by about half the students do the best job in spreading out students' scores. That's an important point, so let me make it in a slightly different way: What the developers of traditional standardized achievement tests want are lots of items answered correctly by between 40 and 60 percent of the test takers.

If a test item is answered correctly by too many students—for example, by 80 or 90 percent of the students—that item does little to produce score spread. For instance, an item answered correctly by all students would make no contribution whatsoever to the production of score spread on the test. An item answered correctly by more than 80 percent of the students, therefore, rarely gets on the test in the first place. In essence, for a traditional standardized achievement test to function as it was intended to function, the test dare not contain many items that almost all students answer correctly.

Yet here's the catch: the more important a topic is, the more instructional attention teachers will typically give to that important topic. And the more instructional attention the important topic gets, the better that students will perform on test items related to that important, instructionally emphasized topic. But the better that students perform on such items, the more likely it is that those very items will be deleted from the test when it is revised. (And some of today's nationally standardized tests have been revised many, many times.) Thus, there is a strong tendency to eliminate items covering significant, teacher-stressed content from traditionally constructed standardized achievement tests. Tests that are employed to evaluate schools should contain items assessing significant, suitably emphasized content—not esoteric content included because of its ability to create score spread.

Confused Causality

For my money, however, a third shortcoming of using standardized tests for school evaluation is the most serious. Stating this reason simply, it's impossible to tell what really caused students' test scores.

If you were to spend much time analyzing the actual items that make up today's standardized achievement tests, you'll find three fairly distinctive types of items, only one of which measures what should be taught at school. To clarify what I mean, I'm going to show you some "representative" items taken from several currently used nationally standardized achievement tests that I've modified only slightly, in unimportant ways, to maintain test security.

The first item on page 71 is a straightforward subtraction problem that any typical fourth grader will have encountered. Although there's always the possibility that a test's items won't satisfactorily match what's supposed to be taught in a given community, items such as this subtraction example do in fact measure what's taught in school.

Yet there's a second kind of item you'll find on traditional standardized achievement tests, such as the following illustration that in the main, measure students' *inherited academic aptitudes* such as children's innate verbal, quantitative, and spatial aptitudes. The second item on page 71

$$
\begin{array}{r}
863 \\
- \, 668 \\
\hline
\end{array}
\qquad
\begin{array}{l}
\text{A. 205} \\
\text{B. 195} \\
\text{C. 185} \\
\text{D. 295}
\end{array}
$$

A fourth-grade mathematics item.

measures the ability to mentally fold letters in order to find the correct answer. In this case, the correct choice is the letter *B*—that is, choice C. But please realize that what's being assessed here is a child's inherited spatial aptitude, not what's supposed to be taught in school. How many sensible teachers spend instructional time having their students engage in make-believe letter bending? You'd expect to find such items on an intelligence test, because they dominantly measure the academic capacities with which children were born. And children, depending on how lucky they

Which letter below, when folded in half, will have two parts that match exactly?

Z   **F**   **B**   **S**

(A)   (B)   (C)   (D)

A fourth-grade spatial visualization item.

were during the gene-pool lottery, do differ in their quantitative, verbal, and spatial aptitudes.

You might ask why test developers would use such inheritance-linked items in an achievement test. After all, the chromosomes a child inherits hardly constitute what a child has learned. The answer to that question is pretty straightforward: children's inherited spatial, verbal, and quantitative aptitudes are nicely spread out. Thus, test items linked to children's present-at-birth aptitudes are almost certain to produce considerable score spread for a test. But it should be apparent that items linked to kids' inherited aptitudes tend to measure what children *bring to* school rather than what they have learned there. Such items are more fit for intelligence tests than for achievement tests. And yet, if you were to review a standardized achievement test's items carefully, you'll find far more of these inheritance-linked items than you'd expect.

Let's look, then, at the final type of item you'll find on a traditionally constructed standardized achievement test. In the following fifth-grade reading-vocabulary item, the student is asked to read the shaded sentence at the top, then pick the sentence below it in which the underlined word, *field*, is used in the same way as it was above. The correct answer, of course, is D. But, on average, will children from advantaged or disadvantaged backgrounds be more likely to do well on this vocabulary item?

You have probably concluded that advantaged kids will have a built-in edge on this item. If so, you'd be correct. Think about it: if you're a child

---

My dad's <u>field</u> is computer graphics.

A.   The pitcher could <u>field</u> his position.

B.   We prepared the <u>field</u> by plowing it.

C.   The doctor examined my <u>field</u> of vision.

D.   What <u>field</u> will you enter after college?

A fifth-grade reading-vocabulary item.

and one (or both) of your parents is a physician, a journalist, or an attorney, you have a parent who has a "field." If, on the other hand, your dad works in a car wash and your mom is a cashier in a convenience store, you don't have a parent who has a "field." Your parents have *jobs* but not *fields*. Sure, some poor kids will answer such a vocabulary item correctly and some affluent kids won't. But, on average, children whose families have a higher socioeconomic status (SES) will do better on test items similar to the one you just saw.

And, once more you might ask why test developers would use these sorts of SES-linked items in an achievement test. Same question, same answer. Items that are linked to SES do a great job in producing score spread. You see, SES is a variable that's nicely spread out, and it doesn't change all that rapidly. SES-linked items definitely help spread out kids' test scores. But SES-linked items, as was true with inheritance-linked items, measure what children bring to school, not what they learn there.

Are there many inheritance-linked or SES-linked items on today's nationally standardized achievement tests? I recently reviewed two of those tests at a single grade level, item by item, and found that, in reading, about 50 percent of the items were either aptitude-linked or SES-linked; in language arts it was more than 75 percent! In math the figure was only around 15 percent. While I tried to be quite objective in reviewing the items, if you were to divide my percentages in half that still leaves far too many items on standardized achievement tests, especially in reading and language arts, that measure what kids bring to school. And remember, even the items on these tests that actually measure what ought to be taught in school may not turn out to match the particular curriculum content that's supposed to be taught in a given locality.

As we've seen, then, there are three reasons that off-the-shelf, nationally standardized achievement tests shouldn't be used to evaluate schools. Even if the tests' publishers have added some items to better match a state's curriculum, standardized achievement tests are instructionally insensitive. When such tests are employed for that purpose, they're certain to produce misleading estimates of a school staff's effectiveness. If a school's staff is supposed to improve students' test scores each year in order to hit that year's AYP target, and the test being used is incapable of detecting even significant instructional improvements, how can teachers possibly beat the AYP game? The answer is simple: they can't.

In many of our states, however, the tests apt to be used for NCLB implementation will not be nationally standardized, off-the-shelf, achievement tests. Instead, customized tests will have been built within a given state to better match that state's curriculum. Yet these customized tests have often been constructed by the very same testing companies that build and sell the five national standardized achievement tests. As a consequence, many customized state accountability tests have been constructed in a very traditional way—that is, in a way that focuses on producing sufficient score spread to permit norm-referenced comparisons among students.

If your state is intending to use customized accountability tests for purposes of NCLB assessment, you need to find out if those tests were constructed using traditional, spread-the-scores procedures. If so, it's likely that your state's customized accountability tests may not produce accurate school evaluations as required in NCLB.

While we all want to know whether students are learning what they're supposed to, traditionally constructed standardized tests—tests that seek score spread in order to provide comparative scores—are not the answer.

It is possible, however, to build nontraditional standardized achievement tests, tests that can give us accountability evidence but also can provide teachers with well-described instructional targets. Given such tests, there would be little need for curriculum cuts, excessive drilling, or item-focused preparation. Using appropriate standardized achievement tests, accountability evidence can be supplied at the same time that instruction is being improved. This can be a rare but important instance of having one's cake and eating it too. You'll learn about such tests in chapter 7. Next, however, in chapter 6, I want to look at the second type of instructionally insensitive test often encountered today.

6

Today's Standards-Based Tests*

When I was a high school teacher in Oregon some time ago my fellow teachers and I at Heppner High School organized our lessons around *goals* or *objectives*. These goals or objectives simply identified the skills or knowledge we wanted our students to learn. Goals were more general statements of our instructional intentions—for instance: "Students will understand how our nation's government functions." Objectives were more specific statements of our instructional intentions, such as: "Students will be able to describe the steps that must be followed if a federal bill is to become a law." In plain talk, goals and objectives, at that time, identified what we wanted our students to learn.

A NEW DESCRIPTOR FOR WHAT
STUDENTS SHOULD LEARN

During the past decade or so, American educators have latched onto a new label to describe what they want their students to learn. That label is

---

*Substantial segments of this chapter are adapted, with permission, from an article by the author appearing in the February 2003 issue of the *American School Board Journal*: "The Trouble with Testing," copyright 2003, National School Boards Association, all rights reserved.

75

content standards. A content standard, then, is today's way of describing the skills and knowledge that students should master. It is interesting to speculate about how a perfectly serviceable pair of labels (*goals* and *objectives*) came to be replaced with *content standards*.

My guess is that it all started when American educators began playing fast and loose with the term *standard*. A *content standard*, it was argued, could describe the skills and knowledge that educators want students to achieve. Although my dictionary offers nearly thirty definitions of the word *standard*, not one of those definitions even remotely approximates a description of the skills and knowledge that students are supposed to acquire.

To be frank, I'm really not certain when it was that U.S. educators began to describe their curricular aspirations as content standards; it was probably about ten or fifteen years ago. But I have a strong hunch regarding why they did so. *Standards*, in the traditional way that this noun has been used—and especially if it is preceded by the adjective *high*—is instantly transformed into a commodity that simply reeks of goodness. Who, in their right mind, could ever be opposed to high standards? If the nation's educators claimed that they were setting out to promote students' mastery of high standards, who would dare criticize such a laudable aspiration? High standards is a term that, by definition alone, elicits approval.

Thus, when the phrase *standards-based assessment* subsequently found its way into educators' conversations, it too was positively perceived. Standards-based assessment was touted as an approach to determining whether students had mastered all sorts of commendable skills and knowledge—that is, commendable content standards. Moreover, because such an assessment approach was supposedly based on those commendable content standards, there was a clear implication that standards-based tests would surely assist teachers in their efforts to promote students' mastery of the content standards those teachers were supposed to be promoting.

In many instances, for example, a state's curriculum officials first identified a set of content standards for their state, then statewide standards-based tests (either built or bought) were used in an attempt to assess students' mastery of those state-sanctioned content standards. However, despite the alluring approach to curriculum-rooted assessment that's apparently embodied in standards-based testing, in most instances this form of educational assessment has flopped. Let's see why.

FAR TOO MANY CONTENT STANDARDS

Let's suppose that a state's education leaders have formally approved sets of skills and knowledge that constitute the state's officially sanctioned content standards. Suppose further that a state's education officials have installed statewide standards-based tests that are intended to measure students' mastery of those official, state-sanctioned content standards. If both these events were to take place (and they already have in about half of our states), then it would be reasonable to assume that the state's curricular aims were, indeed, being measured by the statewide standards-based tests. That very plausible assumption, however, is usually unwarranted.

PARTISAN CONTENT SPECIALISTS

Much of the problem stems from the enormous number of content standards that are almost always staked out by a state's curriculum specialists. Remember, these curriculum specialists are, in every sense of the term, specialists. And most specialists simply adore their fields of specialization. It's only natural. Thus, for instance, when a state-convened panel of twenty-five mathematics teachers and mathematics curriculum experts is directed to determine what mathematics content the state's students should master, you can safely predict that those mathematics specialists will want the state's students to learn *everything*—that is, everything even remotely mathematical.

And that's why many states have, at this point in time, approved literally hundreds of content standards in a variety of fields to be mastered by students at given grade levels. Sometimes a state's curricular architects may appear to have adopted a much smaller number of content standards—for instance, only a dozen or so fairly broad content standards per grade level. However, closer inspection of those content standards will often reveal that beneath each of the dozen broad curricular aims, there lurk numerous "benchmarks," "indicators," "expectancies," or some similar descriptors. And it is only these more specific descriptions of skills and knowledge that turn out to be stated at a level of clarity suitable for the state's teachers to devise appropriate classroom instructional activities. As a consequence, even if a modest number of supergeneral content standards are being used, beneath those standards there are still way too many curricular aims for teachers to successfully promote in a given school year. Similarly, there are way too many curricular aims to assess in the hour or so typically available for the administration of any standards-based test.

SAMPLING UP A STORM

What, then, do those who must construct standards-based tests typically do when faced with this all-to-common situation? The answer is that they *sample*—that is, they end up measuring some, but not all, of their state's sprawling collection of content standards. This means, of course, that in a given year's state tests, many state-sanctioned content standards are left unmeasured. Yet, the image is often fostered by educational leaders that a state's standards-based assessments actually measure the state's complete array of content standards. That's just not true.

To make matters worse, most worthwhile content standards can't be meaningfully assessed with only one or two items. Yet, this is what usually happens to those content standards that, having come up winners in the sampling sweepstakes, are actually measured on a state test. Such less than complete measurement of curricular aims might be better described as "tokenism-based" rather than "standards-based."

Some commercial test publishers, of course, have claimed that, to a very considerable extent, their off-the-shelf standardized achievement tests are already sufficiently "aligned" with a given state's content standards. It is often in the self-interest of test publishers for a state's potential test adopters to regard a test as being more aligned with a state's content standards than is actually the case. Any alignment study conducted by those who have a special interest in the study's outcome should be regarded as just what it is—a special-interest alignment study. In today's high-stakes testing arena, where enormous numbers of dollars find their way to those firms whose tests are adopted, state decision makers must be particularly wary of such alignment claims.

Even if certain content standards are assessed in one year's state test, while other content standards are assessed in another year's test, for any particular year there is no satisfactory picture available of how students are doing with respect to a state's full range of approved content standards. In almost all instances, today's standards-based tests fail to measure the full set of content standards on which they are supposedly based. And, sadly, those content standards that are actually addressed in a standards-based test are usually measured in only a perfunctory fashion. Yet the proponents of a particular state's standards-based tests seem to promote the perception that all of the state's curricular aims are being assessed each year. It is simply not so.

Teachers, who are under great pressure to boost their students' scores on high-stakes tests, are thus forced to play a guessing game regarding *which* content standards will be assessed on a given year's standards-based tests. Based on a teacher's best guesses, the teacher then supplies instruction to students focused on the teacher-chosen content standards. Unfortunately, more often than not, teachers' guesses about which content standards are to be measured on a given year's test will turn out to be wrong. Students will have studied content that isn't assessed, and students will not have studied content that is assessed. What a muddleheaded way to run a measurement program! And yet, in a number of our states, it appears that officials are going to try to satisfy NCLB assessment requirements by using guessing-game standards-based tests.

Most of the states that are attempting to use customized, state-developed standards-based tests have installed tests built on *mushy* assessment targets. The state's educators, and the state's citizens, truly do not know what's going to be assessed each year.

It is time for educational assessors to stop implying that a state's standards-based tests actually assess a state's too-numerous content standards. To pretend that a few tests, administered in an hour or two, can satisfactorily measure a state's excessively ambitious curricular aspirations is little more than hypocrisy.

As fate would have it, in late 2003 I spent two one-week visits, back to back, in two of our more heavily populated states. I learned almost more than I wanted to about both states' NCLB tests. Both states were currently employing standards-based tests to satisfy NCLB, but in both states those tests were about as instructionally unsound as such tests get. Both states had far too many content standards for teachers to attend to, and neither state supplied results to teachers in a form with which the teachers could make any instructional sense out of their students' performances. However, one of the states had decided to "stand pat" with its weak standards-based tests while the other state was getting underway with the installation of more instructionally sensitive tests. Thus, in one of those states, educators were destined to fail—and fail in droves. In the other state, a move toward more defensible NCLB tests offered educators at least a chance to succeed, and thereby a chance to provide better instruction for the state's students. The contrast between the assessment visions encountered in those almost-adjacent states was considerable.

WRETCHED REPORTING PROCEDURES

If a state's content standards set forth the skills and knowledge to be learned by the state's students, then an instructionally sensible standards-based test ought to provide information regarding which standards have been well taught and which standards haven't. How else can the state's teachers identify the parts of their instruction that ought to be fixed or the parts that are just fine as they are? That's where another deficit in today's standards-based tests becomes all too apparent. Almost always, today's standards-based assessments do not yield standard-by-standard results, either for districts, schools, or individual students.

Instead, what's usually reported is an overall score for, say, mathematics or reading. Occasionally there are attempts to provide some sort of sub-category reports. For instance, a score report might list a student's reading subscores dealing with the student's mastery of fictional or nonfictional reading materials. Even with such subcategory reporting, how much instructional-planning benefit do teachers derive from discovering that their students seem to do better in reading nonfiction than fiction? Today's standards-based tests rarely provide teachers, students, or students' parents with the sort of diagnostically meaningful results with which appropriate instructional decisions can be made.

What instructional sense can a teacher make out of a total "mathematics" score, or even an "algebra" subscore? If a standards-based assessment is going to help teachers do a better job of teaching their students, then that assessment must supply teachers with the kinds of information regarding students' status that allows those teachers to tell which aspects of their instruction are terrific and which aspects are tawdry. Currently, the nation's standards-based tests just don't do so. Putting it another way, almost all of today's standards-based tests rely on *mushy* reporting procedures—procedures that, from an instructional perspective, are downright dysfunctional.

But where our current standards-based assessment situation gets even worse is when many standards-based assessors are loudly claiming that their tests are meaningfully supportive of the educational process. Those claims are blatantly false.

STANDARDS-BASED TESTS AND NCLB

I hope that I have convinced you that the sorts of standards-based tests currently used in so many of our states will subvert, not strengthen, the positive educational aspirations that are embodied in NCLB. I know that it seems to make sense, on the surface, for NCLB assessments to be standards-based tests. After all, NCLB tests are supposed to be based on a state's challenging content standards. But, if folks really care about what happens to kids in classrooms, on-the-surface assessment doesn't cut it.

In addition, NCLB spells out clearly that a state's NCLB tests must "produce individual student interpretive, descriptive, and diagnostic reports . . . that allow parents, teachers, and principals to understand and address the specific academic needs of students. . ." So, federal lawmakers clearly intended for a state's NCLB tests to provide student-level diagnostic information. But if there is no feedback at a level that teachers can act on the information, how can the tests be diagnostic?

What people must find out is whether a particular standards-based test, the one used in their state, is likely to promote better learning in the classroom. If it does, then that standards-based test is appropriate for implementing NCLB. You see, it will be impossible for educators to provide test-based evidence of progress by their students if the tests being used are the sorts of standards-based tests I've been panning so far in this chapter. And if a school's annual improvement targets are not attained, of course, that school fails as far as adequate yearly progress (AYP) assessments are concerned. If the wrong tests are being used in a state, however, then that "failing" label is likely to be undeserved.

Let's recognize that if standards-based tests are mushy up front and mushy at the end, those tests will be every bit as instructionally insensitive as the standardized achievement tests described in chapter 5. Double-mush standards-based tests, sadly, are currently being used in many states as their response to NCLB accountability requirements. Double-mush NCLB tests are a big mistake.

Using most of today's standards-based tests to satisfy NCLB is no more sensible than using traditionally constructed standardized achievement tests to do so. Neither of these assessment approaches yields an accurate picture of how much instructional progress is really taking place in a school or in a school district. And the heart of the NCLB-based approach to educational accountability, of course, hinges on how much annual improvement is seen in students' scores on NCLB-decreed statewide tests.

You've now learned that two types of widely used tests won't work for NCLB assessment. Will any sort of achievement test do the job, or is this an assessment problem without a solution? Fortunately, standards-based tests *can* work if they are deliberately constructed in a way that both supplies accurate accountability information for school evaluation and, at the same time, helps teachers do a better instructional job. Such standards-based tests can help NCLB achieve its intention of getting many more of our students to learn what they ought to be learning. These sorts of tests can supply accurate information on which to base AYP. You'll learn about such tests in the next chapter.

7

Instructionally Supportive
Accountability Tests

As you have seen in the previous two chapters, it is altogether senseless to evaluate the quality of a school's teachers by using either (1) traditionally constructed standardized achievement tests or (2) double-mush standards-based tests. Neither kind of test is instructionally sensitive. Neither kind of test provides the evidence that can tell parents and educators whether a school's staff is truly making adequate yearly improvements.

That's where we stand. Now what's to be done about it? The answer is straightforward. We need to install NCLB tests that do, indeed, provide accurate evidence of students' achievement. Such tests would provide the sorts of student test scores that allow us to know when a school is determined to be "failing," whether this is an accurate label for the school. But we also need NCLB tests that will stimulate improvements in education, not a deterioration in educational quality. In short, we need other kinds of achievement tests. We need *instructionally supportive accountability tests*.

AN INDEPENDENT COMMISSION'S DELIBERATIONS

In chapter 1, I suggested that in the 2000 presidential campaign both the Republican and the Democratic nominees had stressed the need for increased accountability testing in U.S. public schools. A number of my colleagues and I, familiar with some of the negative educational consequences linked to certain sorts of high-stakes tests, were apprehensive about what would most likely be (after a new president's election) the expanded use of high-stakes tests and, therefore, an even greater negative impact of such testing.

Accordingly, well in advance of congressional accord regarding the specifics of NCLB, a group of five national associations of educators appointed a commission of ten experts who, because of their conversance with both assessment and instruction, might offer suggestions regarding how any new federally required accountability tests could have a positive rather than negative impact on our public schools.[4]

Thus, the ten-member Commission on Instructionally Supportive Assessment was formed in mid-2001.[5] Members of the commission agreed to tackle this task without remuneration as long as the five sponsoring organizations did not alter the commission's conclusions. Because the five sponsoring organization abided by that agreement, the commission was allowed to arrive at its recommendations independently. It issued two reports in October 2001, both of which are available on the websites of any of the five national groups who supported our work.[6] Although—because I chaired this commission—I could be accused of bias, nonetheless I regarded my nine fellow commission members as a particularly astute group of testing and teaching specialists. Briefly, here are our conclusions and how we arrived at them.

Our task, as we saw it, was to describe the kinds of large-scale achievement tests that would simultaneously (1) provide score-based accountability information needed to evaluate the quality of a state's schools and (2) help a state's teachers do a better job of instructing their students. We recognized that there would almost certainly soon be federal legislation calling for an expanded use of test-based accountability, and we regarded that likelihood as altogether appropriate. Indeed, members of the commission believed that suitable high-stakes achievement tests could help, not harm our schools. However, we feared that instructionally insensitive tests would be employed to hold U.S. educators accountable. If our fears materialized, then the right accountability game would be played, but it would be misplayed because the wrong score-keeping tools were being used.

As a group, members of the commission recognized that the overarching purpose of any educational accountability program is to make classroom instruction more effective—so that more children will learn what they ought to be learning. Our commission, therefore, set out to identify the sorts of tests that would stimulate improved classroom instruction while also supplying the necessary accountability evidence for school-by-school evaluations.

Looking at the Options

Early on in our discussions, commission members concluded that traditionally constructed standardized achievement tests, because of their comparative assessment mission and their need to create sufficient score spread, would not fill the bill. Such tests would not be sufficiently sensitive to the effects of instruction so that effective schools could be accurately distinguished from ineffective schools. In too many instances, such tests would measure the composition of the student body that was enrolled in a school, not the effectiveness with which those students had been taught. No, our commission concluded that traditionally constructed tests—tests designed to yield norm-referenced inferences—would be appropriate neither for accountability purposes nor for helping teachers do a better instructional job.

Commission members were, however, positively disposed toward the fundamental measurement notion underlying standards-based tests. We recognized that any sort of appropriate accountability test ought to be linked directly to the state-approved curricular targets at which a state's teachers were supposed to be aiming their instruction. Nevertheless, we concluded that almost all the standards-based tests commonly employed in the United States, with the important exception of those tests intended to assess students' composition skills, were instructionally flawed.

First, as you've seen, because most states' existing standards-based tests attempted to measure an enormous collection of curricular targets, teachers were typically obliged to guess at the content standards that would actually be assessed in any year's statewide test. In other words, existing standards-based tests did not describe with sufficient clarity just what it was that those tests would be assessing each year. Commission members knew that teachers can't plan instruction to improve students' to-be-assessed skills and knowledge if teachers don't have a lucid idea about what the to-be-assessed skills and knowledge actually are.

A second equally serious shortcoming of existing standards-based tests, as seen by the commission, was that no meaningful feedback was typically supplied to teachers, students, or students' parents about which assessed curricular aims had or hadn't been mastered. The inability of current standards-based tests to supply such feedback, of course, stems chiefly from the attempts of such tests to measure far too many content standards.

It was thus clear to the commission members that neither traditional achievement tests nor the sorts of standards-based tests currently being used in the United States would be suitable for satisfying the dual missions of accountability and instruction enhancement. We argued, therefore, for the creation of instructionally supportive accountability tests.

The Commission's Solution

The commission organized its report around a series of nine "requirements" that we believed must be satisfied in order for an accountability assessment program to be instructionally supportive. Among these requirements were the use of standards-based tests that (1) measure students' mastery of a much smaller number of extraordinary significant content standards; (2) provide sufficiently clear descriptions regarding what was being assessed so that teachers, students, and their parents would understand what was to be tested; and (3) report test results so that an individual student's per-standard status could be determined. (In my view, those three requirements are the most important of the commission's nine requirements. As noted above, complete discussion of any of these requirements and a copy of our reports can be downloaded from the websites of any of the five sponsoring organizations.) Let's first look briefly at the reasoning underlying each of these three requirements. Later, we'll consider the remaining requirements set forth by the commission.

Requirement 1: Prioritized Curricular Aims

Our commission recognized that it was folly to attempt to measure students' mastery of hundreds of curricular aims (that is, content standards) in the hour or two that statewide tests typically take. Thus, our first requirement calls for instructionally supportive accountability tests to be focused on a much smaller number of curricular targets. So, instead of a standards-based test that tries to measure students' mastery of thirty or forty content standards, we believe such tests should focus on measuring only a half-dozen or even fewer content standards.

Of course, if an instructionally supportive accountability test is going to measure only a handful of curricular aims, then those aims must be supersignificant. A good example of the kind of content standard the commission members had in mind would be "a student's ability to compose original narrative, explanatory, and persuasive essays." This is a single skill, but an extremely powerful one that incorporates a number of necessary subskills—such as a student's ability to employ appropriate spelling, punctuation, and grammar in order to generate different sorts of original essays. Similar, powerful skills can be isolated in reading and mathematics.

In some instances, movement toward instructionally supportive accountability tests will require the alteration of a state's existing content standards so that a number of smaller-scope content standards can be coalesced under larger-scope, yet still measurable, content standards. In other settings, the existing content standards need not be changed. However, from the more important of those standards, an assessment framework could be derived for NCLB tests. That framework, demonstrably drawn from already approved content standards, might then focus on only a handful of patently important curricular aims.

Here's the way our commission put it:

Requirement 1: A state's content standards must be prioritized to support effective instruction and assessment.

Because

- Educators in many states cannot adequately address within the amount of time available for instruction the large number of content standards that are supposedly measured by state tests.
- State tests often do not adequately assess all of the content standards, and frequently center on standards that are easiest to assess.
- State tests rarely provide educators with the kind of information they need to improve instruction.

Requirement 2: Clearly Described Content Standards

The commission's second requirement is closely linked to its first. If instructionally supportive accountability tests are going to measure only a modest number of super-significant content standards, then it is obviously important that teachers understand what those assessment targets really are. Unfortunately, most state's official content standards are often stated in a fashion that is far from clear. (Ambiguously stated content standards are the rule, not the exception.) Thus, accompanying every instructionally supportive accountability test should be a relatively brief, clear description of each curricular aim to be measured. These descriptions should be written in straightforward language so that teachers can readily recognize the essence of what's being assessed, hence what needs to be promoted instructionally. Teachers are pressed for time, and they just don't have the time to wade through lengthy and complicated descriptions of what an NCLB test is supposed to be measuring. Therefore, the descriptions of what's to be assessed must definitely be short enough and clear enough to be teacher palatable. Ideally, from the descriptions for teachers, even shorter and more readable descriptions of the to-be-assessed content standards should be developed for both students and for their parents. As the commission wrote:

> **Requirement 2:** **A state's high-priority content standards must be clearly and thoroughly described so that the knowledge and skills students need to demonstrate competence are evident.**

Because

- A state's high-priority content standards will be measured by state tests.
- Educators must understand what each of these content standards calls for from students.
- Many content standards are not worded with sufficient clarity for rigorous instructional planning and assessment design.

Requirement 3: Per-Standard Reporting

The third requirement of the commission rounds out what is clearly necessary if an accountability test is going to improve instruction. If teachers find out what things are significant enough to be assessed (Requirement 1), and understand those things well enough to aim instruction accurately at them (Requirement 2), then it is imperative to let teachers know whether their instruction has worked. Accordingly, the third requirement of the commission calls for results of an instructionally supportive accountability test to be reported on a standard-by-standard basis so that teachers, students, and students' parents find out *which* content standards have or have note been mastered by students. Without this sort of per-standard feedback, the curriculum–instruction–assessment feedback loop (identified in chapter 4) ceases to function.

Remember, though, that this requirement of the commission refers to content standards, but only when those content standards are stated at a level of clarity needed for teachers' instructional planning. Thus, if in a state you find *content standards* stated so generally that teachers need to move to a more specific set of descriptors such as *benchmarks*, then this commission recommendation should be interpreted as calling for *benchmark-by-benchmark* reporting.

In order to supply per-standard reports, of course, it is frequently necessary to employ a sufficient number of test items to get an accurate fix on a student's status with respect to a given content standard. For instance, if a test uses multiple-choice items to assess a student's ability to perform a certain kind of mathematical operation (such as long division), it may take the answers to ten or more items for teachers to arrive at a reasonably valid inference about a student's mastery of that skill. Because more items are often needed to supply per-standard feedback, this is yet another reason for the emphasis on assessing only a small number of high-priority standards.

It is far better to accurately assess a modest number of well-described and properly reported curricular aims than it is to inaccurately assess a large number of poorly described and unclearly reported curricular aims. If classroom teachers can't determine which parts of their instructional program are purring and which parts are sputtering, how can those teachers know what needs fixing and what doesn't? Similarly, if parents can't find out which skills their children haven't truly mastered, how can those parents pitch in and help? Here's how our commission justified this point:

Requirement 3: **The results of a state's assessment of high-priority content standards should be reported standard-by-standard for each student, school, and district.**

Because

- Students, parents, educators, and policy makers need information about which content standards students are and are not attaining.
- Educators can do little to improve students' achievement without information about their performance on each high-priority content standard.

Requirement 4: Optional Classroom Assessments

The commission members recognized that an emphasis on a small number of important curricular targets could engender even more flagrant curriculum reductionism than students have seen in recent years. Clearly, attempts must be made to counter such an educationally unsound consequence. Accordingly, the commission added a pair of requirements specifically intended to diminish such curricular reductionism. The first one deals with optional classroom assessments intended to measure important content standards that are unassessed by a state's accountability tests. With this requirement the commission wanted to increase the likelihood that teachers would address curricular aims that, though worthwhile, would not be measured on such accountability exams as a state's NCLB tests. The commission outlined this fourth requirement as follows:

Requirement 4: **A state must provide educators with optional classroom assessment procedures that can measure students' progress in attaining content standards not assessed by state tests.**

Because

- Content standards that are not assessed by state tests are important and should be given instructional attention.
- Educators need good assessment tools to monitor students' achievement and rarely have the time and resources to develop such tools.

- Assessments that are routinely administered by educators can and should be used to provide a complete picture of what students know and are able to do.

In passing, I should note that since the publication of our commission's October 2001 reports, several of the commission members have recognized a deficiency with this requirement. It would have been preferable for us to have also advocated the provision of optional classroom assessments that measured those content standards *that were assessed* by a state's accountability tests. These classroom assessments would make it possible for teachers to determine their students' en-route progress toward those state-assessed content standards. Thus, for example, even before the administration of a state's NCLB tests in spring of the school year, the state's teachers could easily find out how well their students were mastering those NCLB-assessed skills. And, of course, if additional instruction was indicated, teachers could supply it.

Requirement 5: Monitoring Curricular Breadth

Another effort by the commission to counteract the potential curricular reductionism apt to be fostered by assessments measuring a smaller number of prioritized content standards was to require a state to formally monitor, using quantitative and/or qualitative methods, the degree to which a state's educators were devoting instructional attention to content standards or to subject areas not measured by the state's accountability tests. We were convinced that curricular attention to such key areas as music, art, and physical education has dangerously diminished. Indeed, even in main-line subject areas such as language arts, instructional time for state-untested content is often disappearing. We recognized that different states would choose to carry out such monitoring in different ways. But we wanted to see the installation of at least some formal monitoring mechanism aimed at countering curricular reductionism. As the commission explained:

> *Requirement 5:* **A state must monitor the breadth of the curriculum to ensure that instructional attention is given to all content standards and subject areas, including those that are not assessed by state tests.**

Because

- Students benefit from a rich and deep curriculum; and state tests that measure high-priority content standards could narrow curricular coverage unless steps are taken to forestall such narrowing.

Other Requirements

The commission also identified several other requirements for instructionally supportive assessment. In order to take full instructional advantage of this new breed of accountability tests, the commission suggested providing teachers with ample professional development. Another requirement urged that there be continuing evaluation of the impact of any accountability system relying on instructionally supportive tests to make sure those tests have a positive impact on children. The remaining two commission requirements dealt with the time that should be allowed for development of a statewide instructionally supportive accountability test and how to assure that all children, including those with disabilities and special needs, are assessed with instructionally supportive tests. Especially since the release of NCLB regulations permitting no more than one percent of a state's disabled students to be given alternate tests, the commission's sixth requirement seems particularly important. The commission urged that accountability tests be developed from the very beginning so they are as suitable as possible for assessing *all* children. Assessment experts who work with special groups of youngsters usually refer to this as *universally designed assessment.* As noted earlier, the commission's reports are available online from any of the five associations that sponsored our deliberations.

WELL-SUITED FOR NCLB

Our commission wanted American educators to be accountable for their efforts. However, the commission also wanted those educators to do an improved job of instructing students. We believe that NCLB has a reasonable chance of accomplishing both of those goals, *but only if it is implemented by a state's adoption of instructionally supportive accountability tests.* Such tests will give educators a reasonable chance to succeed. Such tests will provide parents with a more defensible picture of the quality of their children's schools. Such tests will help children learn.

PART III

Evaluating Schools

8

The Evidence Needed
to Evaluate Schools

It makes sense that people want to know whether our nation's schools are doing a good job. This is especially true for parents, who typically want to find out how good a particular school is—specifically, the school that their child attends. However, since the introduction of NCLB, standardized test scores have begun to override all other means of evaluating schools when, in fact, a broader range of evidence is needed. In this chapter you'll learn what sorts of evidence are needed when trying to decide just how effective a particular school really is.

FOUR KINDS OF EVIDENCE

There are four useful sources of evidence regarding a school's quality, and we'll be looking at each of them in this chapter. First, there is evidence that can be supplied by *instructionally supportive accountability tests*, the type of tests you learned about in the previous chapter. You'll see how such tests can be built so that they're dramatically different from the state-level accountability tests being used today in most states. Second, you'll see how students' *work samples*, such as an original essay, can be carefully collected and scored in order to supply convincing evidence about a school's effectiveness. Third, I'll briefly explain how certain kinds of *affective data*, such as children's attitudes toward school or their confidence in being able to perform particular skills, can also shed light on a school's quality. This will be a light introduction to affective assessment, because in chapter 9 I'll be digging more deeply into this important kind of evidence regarding school quality. And fourth, we'll look at the virtues of *nontest academic indicators*, such as attendance records and tardiness statistics, in determining a school's success. These four kinds of evidence, when used in concert, can provide a reasonably accurate picture of a school's success. Let's start off, then, with the sort of evidence that's obtainable from students' scores on standardized tests.

INSTRUCTIONALLY SUPPORTIVE ACCOUNTABILITY TESTS

As you saw in the previous chapter, an instructionally supportive accountability test (1) is designed to measure a small number of truly significant standards, (2) describes in reasonably clear language just what the test is assessing, and (3) provides standard-by-standard reports regarding students' mastery of these criteria. Technically, such tests are "standards based" in the sense that they are designed to measure students' mastery of a modest number of genuinely significant content standards. But, as you saw in chapter 6, instructionally supportive accountability tests are a far cry from most of today's so-called standards-based tests.

For purposes of evaluating schools, however, any achievement test really needs to be standardized. In other words, the students in different schools must be measured with the same test that's always administered in the same way to all students throughout a state. There should be no "home-court advantage" at any given school. Clearly, then, a state's NCLB tests will be typically standardized—not only because that's required by federal law, but also just because it makes good sense.

A key advantage of an instructionally supportive accountability test is that such a test can simultaneously supply evidence for school evaluation, yet also provide a state's teachers with excellent instructional information.

(As I noted earlier, a few states have been allowed by NCLB officials to try to implement the school evaluation requirements using locally chosen tests. I think that locally chosen tests make substantial sense instruction-ally, but for evaluating a state's schools, I prefer a common yardstick less vulnerable to local manipulation.) For one thing, the state's teachers can do a better job because an instructionally supportive test stakes out clearly the nature of the skills and knowledge that the test is attempting to measure. Moreover, such a test lets teachers know how well their instruction has worked. That's because it is designed so diagnostic data will be provided regarding which students have mastered which content standards.

In many states we now find customized standards-based tests being used that attempt to reflect a state's official content standards. But not all of those state-constructed standards-based tests are instructionally supportive. In states where customized standards-based tests are used, if those tests are not instructionally supportive, then it is likely they are not suitable for evaluating the state's schools according to the provisions of NCLB. State tests that are not instructionally supportive may indeed sat-isfy the legal requirements of NCLB; however, such tests will do little to help achieve that legislation's ultimate goal—namely, the improvement of America's schools.

If the first kind of sensible evidence by which to evaluate schools is students' performance on instructionally supportive accountability tests, ideally, these tests would be administered to students both at the beginning of a school year and also at the end of that same school year. But the administration and scoring of large-scale achievement tests is quite costly, so in most settings there will be only one test administration per year, usually in the spring—toward the end of the school year.

STUDENTS' WORK SAMPLES

In addition to students' scores on statewide achievement tests, another powerful indicator of school quality can be secured by looking at students' locally collected work samples. I have in mind such samples as the narrative essays students write, or the oral reports they give describing experiments they have carried out in a science class. In mathematics, for example, a typical work sample might be a student's written solution of a complex problem requiring not only the application of basic computational skills, but also the use of geometry, measurement, and even a smidgen of statistics. As you can see, the kinds of work samples I'm talking about aren't trivial ones such as the child's completion of worksheets requiring the addition of pairs of two-digit numbers. Rather, I'm referring to work samples that reflect students' mastery of demanding, high-level skills.

Now, because most work samples are far more economical to collect and to score in a school (or in a school district) than would be true at the state level, work samples can often be used locally on a *pretest–posttest* basis with the same children taught by the same teacher. For example, sixth-grade students can be asked to write an explanatory essay at the start of the school year and then another explanatory essay at the end of the school year. Meaningful improvement in the quality of students' pretest-to-posttest essays, if it is present, will suggest that effective instruction has been taking place. Such pretest-to-posttest contrasts can be carried out in each teacher's classroom, and then summarized for an entire school if the school's staff wants to provide an overall picture of the staff's instructional success.

However, to provide *believable* evidence of instructional effectiveness, it is necessary to collect and evaluate students' work samples in a particular way. Suppose you're a middle school English teacher and you want your students to be able to write powerful, persuasive essays. Early in the school year, perhaps in September, you could give your students a performance task such as writing a position paper to persuade city council members to expand the number of city-owned parks. Students are told not to date their essays, and you must supply the paper on which the pretest essays are to be written.

Then, near the end of the school year, possibly in May, you give the identical essay-writing task to your students. You supply the same kind of

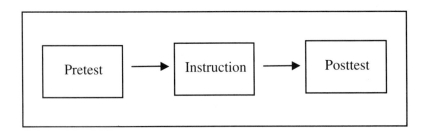

A pretest–posttest design.

paper on which students are to write their undated postinstruction essays. Then you assign a secret code to all the papers so that only you can tell which are pretest and which are posttest essays. At that point, you mix the pretests and posttests together, then ask parents or other nonteachers to judge the quality of each of the essays. You'll usually need to give those scorers a quick course in how to evaluate a persuasive essay's quality, typically using some sort of rubric (scoring guide). There are, incidentally, lots of first-rate rubrics around that deal with the evaluation of students' essays, and parents can quickly learn how to use such rubrics to score the essays.

After the scoring of all the essays has been completed, you then separate the pretest from the posttest essays based on your previous coding of the papers. If your instruction was effective, the bulk of the essays that have been judged to be superior will turn up in the posttest pile. And most of the essays judged to be weaker will have been assigned to the pretest pile—that is, they will have been written by your students before you started your instruction about the writing of persuasive essays. By having nonpartisan judges "blind score" the essays, you'll have produced credible evidence that some first-rate pretest-to-posttest instruction has taken place.

If collected and scored properly, students' work samples can supply solid evidence about whether instruction has been successful. If an analysis of students' properly scored work samples indicates that students have mastered important skills, then it's difficult to conclude that a school is "failing." The more teachers in a school who can produce properly collected and systematically scored work samples demonstrating students' meaningful pretest-to-posttest growth, the more positively a school should be evaluated.

AFFECTIVE DATA

Let's look now at a third kind of evidence that can be used to evaluate schools—namely, affective data. With the term *affective data* I am referring to students' *anonymous* responses to carefully constructed affective inventories usually intended to measure students' attitudes and interests. For example, students might be given a series of statements regarding their interest in certain subjects. The statements might be phrased along such lines as "I really like to read about historical events" or "I find science dull." For each such statement, the student anonymously marks an agree-ment/disagreement response such as "I strongly agree," "I disagree," and so on.

Because these affective inventories are self-report in nature, even if there are no right or wrong answers, a few students may not respond honestly to affective inventories—even though the inventories are completed anonymously. Therefore, affective data should be used only to make interpretations about groups of students, not individual students. That's because the average response of a group of students to an anony-mous, self-reported affective inventory will usually provide a reasonably accurate picture of a student group's affect. (The responses of students who are unusually positive or unusually negative will typically be over-ridden when group averages are computed.)

Affective data can be particularly illuminating with respect to the quality of instruction taking place in a school. Let's say, for example, that based on affective inventories given twice a year, students in a specific school display much more interest in doing free-time reading at the end of the academic year than at the beginning. Perhaps they also show substantially increased confidence in their ability to give oral presentations to their classmates. Those positive increases in students' affect clearly indicate that good things are going on in the school. Conversely, if students' preinstruction to postinstruction affective responses indicate that they are finding school less interesting, more boring, or less safe, this is meaningful negative evidence about a school's educational impact on its students.

Happily, anonymous preinstruction to postinstruction affective data can be collected quite inexpensively. Because students' attitudes toward various aspects of school are educationally important, such affective data can help us decide how effectively a school's staff is functioning. Due to the potential significance for school evaluation of affective evidence, I will treat the collection of affective data more fully in the next chapter.

NONTEST ACADEMIC INDICATORS

Let's look now at the fourth and final kind of evidence that ought to be con-sidered when evaluating a school—namely, nontest academic indicators. Such indicators, because of their relevance to the quality of education provided at a school, can help us decide how successfully that school has been educating its students. For example, the attendance rates at a school, as well as the school's tardiness statistics, certainly relate to the school's effectiveness. If, at a given school, attendance is going down and tardiness is going up, you'd have to think that there are problems of some sort. Conversely, if more and more kids are attending a school's classes, and they're rarely tardy, we can conclude that what's going on there seems to be drawing students to the school, and they're getting to their classes on time.

The particular kinds of nontest academic indicators you'd want to look at will often depend on the specific school involved. In certain schools, for example, you might want to review the amounts of graffiti on campus or the quantities of litter on the school grounds. (Less graffiti and less litter, of course, reflect positively on a school.) In some high schools you could be looking at the number of students who continue their education after graduation, or the number of advanced placement courses taken and passed by the school's students.

The particular nontest academic indicators that will help illuminate a school's effectiveness are those any sensible person would be willing to believe, in fact, reflect on how well a school's staff is doing. Indeed, that's the acid test for all four kinds of evidence we've been considering. Will the evidence help a fair-minded person accurately determine if a school's staff is successfully educating its students?

EVALUATIVE EVIDENCE IN FOUR FLAVORS

You've now considered the four types of evidence introduced to evaluate school quality. Clearly, the importance of each kind of evidence in evaluating schools will depend on the quality of the *particular* evidence at hand. Suppose, for example, that the standardized test scores that were available consisted of students' performances on one of the instructionally *insensitive* standardized achievement tests I described earlier. Because students' performances on such tests are not an accurate reflection of teachers' instructional effectiveness, it would be silly to give great evaluative significance to students' performances on such tests.

Similarly, if the only nontest indicator available for judging schools consists of students' tardiness rates, then I'd be reluctant to assign much importance to that category of evidence. Tardiness data can be important,

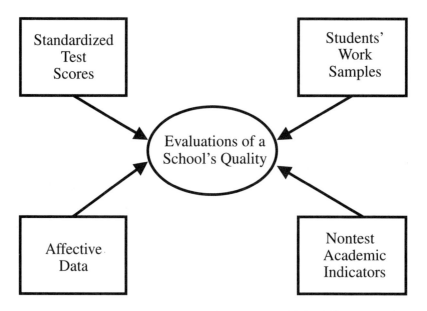

Contributions of four sources of evidence to judgments regarding a school's quality.

of course, but attendance rates are usually far more important. Clearly, the more evidence that's available in one of these four categories, and the more credible the particular evidence is, the more influence it should have when a school's quality is determined.

In this chapter I've been looking at a more defensible way to evaluate schools than a simplistic reliance on tests—and the wrong kinds of tests at that. We have already taken a look at instructionally supportive accountability tests in chapter 7, so there's no need for further treatment of that source of evidence. And, as I indicated earlier, in the next chapter I will familiarize you with the way that affective data should be collected. Then, in chapter 10, I'll try to show you how these four evidence sources can be used to determine whether a particular school should be regarded, in fact, as a failing school.

What's been the impact of all this accountability-inspired pressure on our nation's teachers? Well, it's difficult to drop into any faculty lounge these days and fail to encounter teachers who are complaining not only about the amount of test-induced pressure they personally perceive but, more important, about the adverse effects that high-stakes testing is having on their instruction. Without question, the increased pressures stemming from the need to satisfy NCLB's adequate yearly progress targets will have a great impact on a teacher's classroom activities. The question is, simply, whether that impact will be good or bad. NCLB's spotlight on the quality of specific schools has the potential to alter dramatically what goes on in America's public education. If the stakes were high before, then NCLB is going to send those stakes soaring off the charts. We must all do what we can to ensure that children truly benefit from this influential federal law.

Given this context, parents must demand a full range of legitimate evidence regarding a school's quality. What educators must do, even without being called on, is proactively produce a full range of legitimate evidence regarding a school's quality. That evidence won't be produced by using traditionally constructed standardized achievement tests or by relying on mushy standards-based tests that pretend to measure far too many content standards. But by using other, more appropriate sorts of evidence—the types of evidence considered in this chapter—it really is possible to tell whether our schools are successful.

9

Student Affect

Students' attitudes and interests strongly influence their behavior. In that way, children are not different from adults. Unquestionably, people's attitudes and interests are influential on their actual behaviors. For this reason, I'd like to devote additional attention to the way that evidence of students' attitudes, interests, and values can bear on school evaluations.

I confess right now that I personally believe a school's influence on its students' attitudes, interests, and values is tremendously important. Have you ever watched a group of kindergarten youngsters troop off to school during the early weeks of their first year at school? Those children are almost always loaded with enthusiasm and joy. They love school, and they love to learn. Then, as those same children grow older, the joy that radiated from them as kindergartners begins to evaporate. By the time those former kindergartners hit middle school or high school, their enthusiasm for school has often waned—or disappeared completely. What was delight during the first few years of school has transformed into disdain. While not even a highly skilled collection of teachers are likely to maintain the level of enthusiasm that kindergarteners initially bring to school, wouldn't it be great if a school's staff helped students retain at least a meaningful part of those initially positive feelings regarding school?

THE NATURE OF AFFECT

Most educators these days use the term *affect* to describe students' attitudes, interests, and values. The reason students' affect is so important is that it is highly predictive of students' future behavior. Note in the figure below that students' current affective status is highly predictive (but, of course, not perfectly predictive) of students' future behavior. Future behavior, in this instance, can refer to students' subsequent in-school actions (such as the future elective courses for which a student signs up or, perhaps, the amount of time a student devotes to studying) or out-of-school actions (such as whether an adult votes in local elections or, perhaps, devotes much time to reading about local governmental issues).

Though the predictive power of affective data is not perfect, it really is more influential than many people recognize. Here's an example that may help clarify this point. Let's suppose you find out that at School X there is evidence indicating that fully 90 percent of the school's students really enjoy reading. In contrast, over at School Y, evidence indicates that only 35 percent of the students in that school truly enjoy reading. Now, jump ahead about twenty years and make a prediction about whether more of the former students from School X or from School Y will be doing more reading as adults? Probabilistically, there's no doubt about it! On average, those who enjoy reading will—when given the opportunity—engage in more voluntary reading than will those who don't enjoy reading. This is only common sense.

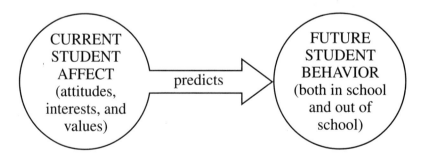

The predictive relationship between students' current affect and their future behavior.

While many affective factors are primarily influenced in the home or by society at large, there are numerous instances in which we find that certain attitudes, interests, and values are shaped almost exclusively in school. Let's look at a few of these.

SCHOOL-RELATED ATTITUDES

Attitudes are *predispositions* to regard something or someone in a particular way. For example, most educators want students to have a positive *attitude toward self*—that is, to possess a positive self-concept. But attitudes toward self are typically influenced most dramatically by what goes on in a child's family. So the school usually ends up playing only a modest role in influencing a child's attitude toward self. There are, of course, exceptions to this general rule. Sometimes a child's personal self-esteem can be dramatically influenced—in a positive or negative direction—by experiences the child has in school.

However, a child's *attitudes toward self as a learner* are much more clearly shaped at school. If children believe they are personally capable of learning, they will tend to tackle learning-related tasks more willingly. After all, such a child will think, "I'm a good learner—and I can do this!" In contrast, children who believe they are not good learners will typically allow that attitudinal predisposition to prevent them from even attempting to learn new things. They will think to themselves, "What's the use of trying? I can't learn something so difficult!"

What a successful school's staff will do, of course, is help as many of its students as possible acquire a positive attitude toward themselves as learners. And to do so, the staff of a successful school will need to make darn sure that the school's students are, in fact, good learners. This means that the school's students must be taught to acquire key reading, writing, and listening skills so that, in truth, they will be able to learn, and to learn well. It also means that children must be taught how to tackle new learning tasks, how to study, how to allocate their time judiciously, and so on. The *instructional* responsibilities that arise when teachers try to influence students' attitudes are not trivial, but the payoffs from modifying an attitude such as students' self-esteem as learners can be enormous. Children who, with reason, believe they are good learners will almost always go on learning. We all tend to engage in those activities that yield success for us. So, good learners continue to learn, even after they leave school. And surely that's what we want for our children.

SCHOOL-RELATED INTERESTS

We have an *interest* in something when it arouses our feelings of concern, attention, or curiosity. If a student is interested in science, for example, then science-related topics will tend to capture the student's attention. Conversely, a student who has little interest in music will, not surprisingly, tend to pay no attention in music class.

To me, one of the worst things that teachers can do is to enable kids to learn a great deal about a subject, but do so in a way that those kids end up hating the subject. Many of today's adult "mathaphobes" became that way because of one or more mathematics teachers who cared more about content mastery than about students' math-related affect. Similarly, while some students who don't have an interest in reading during their school years will surely develop such an interest later, on probability grounds alone, students who are interested in reading during school will be more likely to maintain that interest later in life.

The same might be said about students' interest in biology or art. Think also about children's interests in using computers. You aren't likely to surf around on the Internet if you don't have any interest in getting into that water. Student interests, clearly, are significant.

SCHOOL-RELATED VALUES

Values refer to one's view of what is right, worthwhile, or desirable. When we say that someone "values democracy" we understand that the individual cherishes a form of government in which power is exercised directly by the people or by their freely elected representatives.

Educators need to be exceedingly careful about influencing children's values. That's because the most important values that children acquire—related to such topics as religion, politics, morality, and so on—will fall under the direct responsibility of the home, not the school. However, there are a small number of significant values that can, and should, be addressed in school. Students' *honesty*, for example, is a value whose worth ought to be nurtured in every teacher's classroom. Similarly, *personal integrity* on the part of students—whereby they adhere to their own code of values irrespective of external pressures—is not only important, but can be effectively fostered by teachers. Any values to be promoted by a school's staff, however, must be near-universally accepted by all relevant stakeholders. School staffs should not be dipping into value stews best stirred at home. What that means, in practice, is that affective assessment of students' values should be relatively limited in school.

Because a student's attitudes, interests, and values are so potent in influencing subsequent behavior, it should be self-evident that student affect *could* play a role in evaluating a school's quality. If student affect is (1) appropriately promoted and (2) accurately assessed, I believe it can represent an important factor to be used when evaluating a particular school.

SELECTION OF AFFECTIVE TARGETS

If a school's teachers decide that they wish to promote students' movement toward one or more affective targets, the initial question confronting the staff is "Which affective variables should be addressed?" As you saw in chapter 6 (regarding the deficits of many currently used standards-based tests), it is unwise to focus on too large a number of variables—and that includes curricular aims as well as affective targets. Too many affective targets tend to overwhelm teachers just as surely as too many content standards do. It makes far more sense to focus on only a modest number of significant affective variables than it does to try to address a hoard of affective outcomes. Early on, then, selections need to be made about which affective variables should be promoted in a school's classrooms and, after students' status with respect to those affective variables has been assessed, which affective evidence should play a role in evaluating the school's quality.

A school's staff, if it decides to pursue the promotion of student affect, can arrive unilaterally at its determinations about what affective variables to deal with. However, this situation presents a wonderful opportunity to involve students' parents in this potentially potent evaluative enterprise. An open meeting or two, possibly coupled with some sort of previously "sent home" preference list, could provide a school's faculty with useful insights regarding which affective variables parents would like to see addressed—and which affective variables those parents think *shouldn't* be considered. I need to repeat that affective assessment and instruction dealing with values should be undertaken only if the values involved are approved by all those involved—especially parents.

Let's imagine that such an outreach effort had been undertaken, and that parents' affective preferences meshed rather well with the school faculty's preferences. From such data-gathering activities, it might be concluded that the affective variables to be addressed in a given school year were those cited below. (For the sake of this fictitious illustration, let's assume that we're dealing with an elementary school.)

One Year's Affective Targets

- Students' positive attitudes toward themselves as learners
- Students' interests in science and mathematics
- Students' enjoyment of school
- Students' honesty

Using this hypothetical example, the next thing that the school's faculty would need to do is decide (1) how to move student affect in the desired directions and (2) how to measure any changes in student affect with respect to the selected affective aims.

AFFECTIVELY ORIENTED INSTRUCTION

Yet how do a school's teachers go about modifying student affect? Let's look more carefully at that question. Students have plenty of things that they need to learn in school. There are scads of skills and piles of knowledge that educators want students to acquire. So, the first rule regarding teachers' promotion of affect is that affectively focused instruction must not take up much instructional time. A school's teachers, because they are aware of the affective targets being sought, can usually incorporate—along the way—a number of affectively oriented instructional activities that take little, if any, time away from students' pursuit of key curricular goals.

Let's deal with, for example, the very first of the four fictional outcomes for our hypothetical elementary school—namely, promoting students' positive attitudes toward themselves as learners. What the school's teachers might do here is make certain that students experience many en-route successes as they are learning to master a significant skill or body of knowledge. By setting up a series of gradually more difficult tasks for students, and offering plenty of guided practice plus feedback, most of a teacher's students ought to fare pretty well along the way. And, at the same time, the teacher needs to supply frequent feedback in a form that engenders students' confidence that they have, in fact, been successful in learning these tasks. Such affectively oriented behavior on the teacher's part takes almost no time away from the teacher's regular instructional activities, yet can have a solid impact on students' attitudes toward themselves as learners.

More than you may appreciate, a teacher's awareness of this to-be-assessed affective focus will encourage the teacher to engage in a substantial number of small, but cumulatively important, steps to foster students' more positive regard for themselves as learners. If a given affective target is going to be assessed, you can be certain that such a prospect will keep this target front and center in teachers' minds as they plan their day-to-day classroom activities. While few teachers were trained during their teacher education days regarding how to promote learner affect, affectively focused instructional tactics can be readily mastered by experienced or novice teachers. Teachers can quickly become skilled in mastering affective instructional tactics that, though not particularly time consuming, are apt to be effective.

ASSESSING AFFECT

Now let's turn to the actual collection of evidence regarding students' attitudes, interests, and values. As you'll see, assessing student affect is really rather different from the way that students' skills and knowledge are measured.

Group-Focused Inferences

I hope you'll recall from chapter 4 that educational testing is, at bottom, an enterprise in which educators make assessment-based inferences about a student's unseeable skills and knowledge. Affective measurement also focuses on assessment-based inferences, but inferences about groups of students, not individual students. That's an important difference. What it means, of course, is that a teacher, based on the use of affective assessment instruments, only gets a fix on the affective status of an entire class—and the teacher can never draw an inference about a particular student's affect. Here's why.

Teachers might, in some instances, come up with a reasonably accurate estimate about a particular student's affect based on the teacher's interpretation of the student's classroom behavior. But in many other instances, the teacher's guess about a particular student's unseeable affective status will be as wrong as it can be. Suppose, for example, the affective variable that Mrs. Ballard, a fifth-grade teacher, is concerned about is "students' interest in social studies." Now, during the course of the school year, some students in Mrs. Ballard's fifth-grade class seem to be really interested in Mrs. Ballard's social studies lessons. She notes, with satisfaction, that Maria, one of her students, displays considerable involvement during the treatment of all social studies topics. But, Maria's attention to those topics may actually reflect

- Maria's genuine interest in social studies
- Maria's respect and affection for Mrs. Ballard
- Maria's pursuit of a good grade
- Maria's parents' advice that she "participate" in class

There is ample research showing that human beings, even very small human beings, frequently adopt behaviors that they regard as "socially desirable." In other words, students will often behave in ways that they believe society's adults want them to behave. Thus, when teachers observe a student's in-class behavior, or even a student's out-of-class behavior, those teachers are rarely able to get an accurate reading on that child's true affect. The reality is that teachers typically can't tell about a student's affect simply by observation. Teachers who think they can do so are frequently fooling themselves.

However, even though a teacher cannot be certain about a particular child's attitudes, interests, and values, the teacher can still make great use of information about a student group's affect. For example, suppose a middle school's teachers had decided to emphasize (during the entire school year) "students' confidence in coping with new mathematical problems." If Mr. Hill, a sixth-grade teacher at the school, discovered that his entire class was fearful of dealing with mathematics problems at the start of the school year but was far more confident about dealing with such problems at the end of the first semester, then Mr. Hill can reasonably conclude that his confidence-boosting efforts regarding the solving of math problems seem to be working. Similarly, if Mr. Hill learned that there was *no* presemester to postsemester improvement in his sixth-graders' math-related confidence, he would know that he needed to engage in some different types of confidence-boosting activities. Group-focused inferences about students' affective status can thus be quite instructionally informative to teachers. Such group-focused inferences about students' affect can also be useful when evaluating a school.

Self-Report, Anonymous Affective Inventories

Many of the measurement specialists who have worked on assessing student affect have concluded that the most cost-effective and most accurate way to secure the data needed for making group-focused inferences about students' affect is to employ anonymously completed, self-reported affective inventories. In contrast to a number of more elaborate ways of getting a fix on students' affect (such as, for example, using two-way mirrors to observe students' responses to accomplice-laden staged events), self-reported inventories, if completed with genuine anonymity, almost always work satisfactorily. And, clearly, such self-report affective inventories are much more cost-effective than elaborate affective-assessment procedures.

In order for a self-reported affective inventory to yield accurate group-focused evidence, however, it must be completed anonymously. Not only should the inventory be completed anonymously, but students must perceive that anonymity will be preserved. In other words, students should really believe that their responses cannot be traced back to them. Only if perceptions of true anonymity are present will students—at least most students—supply honest responses.

And this means, of course, that students should definitely not place their names on an affective inventory or, indeed, write any comments at all on such inventories, because they will, with good reason, believe that their handwriting can be used to identify them. Therefore, self-report affective inventories must be completed by students using only checkmarks or X-marks. If a teacher wants to collect additional written comments from students, this should also be done anonymously—but on different self-report inventories that are distributed and collected at a completely different time. Anonymity is the whole game when teachers set out to assess affect.

On page 117, you will find an example of a self-report affective inventory for students in grades four through six. Please note, in the inventory's directions, that care has been taken to let students know their responses are to be genuinely anonymous. If you look closer at the inventory, you'll see that it consists of pairs of statements about particular affective variables; one statement in the pair is positive and one is negative. The pairs of statements deal with students' (1) enjoyment of school in general, as well as their interests in (2) science, (3) composition, (4) reading, (5) oral presentations, (6) mathematics, and (7) social studies. The inventory is based on the hope that students will agree with the positive statement in a particular pair (for instance, will respond that the positive statement in No. 2 regarding science is "very true for me") and disagree with the negative statement in this pair (for instance, will respond that the negative statement regarding science in No. 8 is "not true for me").

Teachers who use an inventory such as the one shown here can get an approximate fix on their students' interest in six subject areas as well as their students' more general enjoyment of school. Even a two-item glimpse of students' affect, from an entire class, can prove useful to teachers. If the teacher wanted to be even more confident about students' affect regarding any particular affective variable, additional statements could be added about that affective variable—for example, four or six statements per variable. However, because affective inventories should never be regarded as "too long" by students, more items per affective variable should usually lead to the deletion of some of the affective variables previously being assessed. If students regard any inventory as excessively long, they will usually give insufficient attention to any of the individual items in such an "unending" inventory.

Even with all this concern about anonymity, will all students respond with complete honesty? Of course not. Even with all that fuss about anonymity, will all students avoid socially desirable responses? Of course not. Even with two, four, or more items per affective variable, can we be absolutely certain of the validity of our affective inferences? Of course not. But, if inventories such as the one above are administered anonymously at the beginning and end of a school year, can we collect enough affective data that will help us evaluate a given school's effectiveness? You bet we can.

Even though some students won't supply honest responses to such inventories, most will. And while it is likely that some students will

SCHOOL AND ME

Directions: Please indicate whether the statements in this inventory are true for you. Some of the statements are positive and some are negative. Decide if each statement is true *for you*. There are no right or wrong answers, so answer honestly. Please do not write your name, or other comments, on the inventory. *Make only X-marks.*

Here is a sample:

	Response (one per statement)		
	Very true for me	**Not true for me**	**I'm not sure**
I *don't* like to watch television.	☐	☒	☐

When you are finished, a student will collect your inventory and place it, along with all other completed inventories, in a sealed envelope that will be taken by the student directly to the principal's office. Thank you for your help.

	Response (one per statement)		
Statements	**Very true for me**	**Not true for me**	**I'm not sure**
1. Most of the time, I like school.	☐	☐	☐
2. I like to learn about scientific things.	☐	☐	☐
3. I can write good reports and stories.	☐	☐	☐
4. I *don't* like to read.	☐	☐	☐
5. I *don't* like to speak in front of the class.	☐	☐	☐
6. I think that doing mathematics is fun.	☐	☐	☐
7. I like when we learn about social studies.	☐	☐	☐
8. I *don't* want to grow up to be a scientist.	☐	☐	☐
9. I really *don't* like to write very much.	☐	☐	☐
10. I like to read books when I have the time.	☐	☐	☐
11. I usually enjoy speaking in front of other students.	☐	☐	☐
12. I *don't* like to do mathematics problems.	☐	☐	☐
13. When we do social studies in school, I *don't* like it.	☐	☐	☐
14. Overall, I *don't* enjoy school very much.	☐	☐	☐

An illustrative self-report affective inventory for a student in grades four through six.

respond too positively (even to an anonymously completed inventory) simply to avoid incurring their teacher's wrath, there will be other students who respond too negatively simply to "get back at their teacher." In general, these sets of too-positive and too-negative responses tend to cancel out one another so that the average response of a group of students, while admittedly approximate, provides a reasonably accurate estimate of a student group's affect.

THE ROLE OF AFFECTIVE DATA
IN SCHOOL EVALUATION

Looking back, then, if affective data can be carefully collected with suitable attention to anonymity, such evidence can play a meaningful role in the evaluation of a particular school. If there is properly collected affective evidence indicating that a school is having a decisively positive impact on its students' affect, as reflected in students' anonymous responses to start-of-school-year versus end-of-school-year affective inventories, then such evidence should definitely be factored into an evaluation of that school. The more substantial the attitudinal shifts and the more significant the affective variables involved, the more attention that should be paid to the affective evidence.

Should affective evidence outweigh test-based data about students' progress in mastering skills or bodies of knowledge? Probably not. Besides, the provisions of NCLB call for primary consideration to be given to the scores earned by students on the state's NCLB-required academic assessments. However, if I weren't sure about a school's success based only on students' achievement test scores, and a set of compelling affective data regarding the school's impact had been presented (either positive or negative), I'd most likely be influenced strongly by such data. For me, affective evidence is significant supplemental evidence of a school's effectiveness.

1 0

Determining a
Particular School's Quality

Now it's time to get specific. Up to this point, you've looked at the way NCLB is to be employed in judging a state's schools, and you've considered the sorts of evidence that can be used to evaluate those schools. In this chapter, you'll be seeing how someone can decide whether a *particular* school should or shouldn't have been given a "failing" label.

In chapter 8, four sources of evidence were identified that can be used to help people arrive at judgments regarding a school's quality. To remind you, those four evidence sources were (1) standardized test scores, (2) students' work samples, (3) affective data, and (4) nontest academic indicators. You've also had an opportunity to consider the kinds of standardized test scores that should or shouldn't be used to evaluate schools. In chapter 9 you learned about how to collect and interpret data regarding students' affect. A bit later in this chapter, I'll ask you to complete three "self-test" exercises in which I'll ask you to evaluate a particular school's quality. Immediately after each of the three exercises, I'll supply you with my thoughts about that exercise. These self-test exercises are intended to provide opportunities for you to do some personal thinking about what's been discussed so far in this book. But before you tackle the self-test exercises, I'd like to expand just a bit more on students' work samples and nontest indicators as sources of evaluative evidence.

STUDENTS' WORK SAMPLES

As a consequence of the instruction that students receive in school, they are supposed to acquire important skills and master significant bodies of knowledge. A work sample is intended to indicate whether students have, indeed, mastered certain skills or bodies of knowledge. Work samples, just as any sort of educational test, allow educators to make inferences (based on what's observable) about students' unobservable skills and knowledge.

What's particularly persuasive about students' work samples is that those samples constitute genuinely compelling evidence about whether kids can or can't do something that's worthwhile. If eighth-grade students are supposed to learn how to write narrative essays in their English classes, and you are looking at an original, especially well-written narrative essay authored by a particular eighth grader at the end of the school year, it is a pretty cut-and-dried inference that this eighth grader has acquired the skill of being able to write narrative essays.

Student work samples are just that—actual samples of a student's work. And if a sample clearly demonstrates that a student has mastered a particular skill or a body of knowledge, then it's difficult to argue that the student hasn't. Conversely, if a student's work sample shows a weak mastery of a skill or body of knowledge, it's hard to argue that the student actually possesses that certain skill or knowledge. The work sample indicates otherwise. Work samples are a potent form of evidence depending on how they are collected and how they are scored. Work samples make it easy for educators (or parents) to make test-based inferences about students' unseeable skills.

For work samples to show that students have learned new things, however, they must be collected on a preinstruction and postinstruction basis. For instance, if Ms. Millen collected students' essays only at the end of a semester, we can't say with certainty the quality of those students' end-of-semester essays is attributable to Ms. Millen's instruction. Even if the essays were really wonderful, we simply don't know whether

Ms. Millen's instructional efforts led to those fine essays or, instead, whether the students were able to write great essays before they were enrolled in Ms. Millen's class. Perhaps the English teacher who taught Ms. Millen's students during the previous school year did a bang-up instructional job as regards essay writing. We just can't tell from posttest assessments alone.

Thus, to get a meaningful fix on what it was that contributed to the quality of students' work samples, it is necessary to collect preinstruction work samples (for instance, during the first few days of a semester or school year) as well as postinstruction work samples (for instance, near the close of a semester or school year). In between this collection of pre- and postinstruction work samples, a teacher's instruction is supposed to be accomplishing its educational magic. It is the contrast between pre- and postinstruction work that allows us to discern whether the teacher's instruction was, in fact, effective or ineffective.

In chapter 8 you also learned that work samples need to be scored in a manner that allows people to make accurate inferences about a teacher's effectiveness. It was recommended that those samples, if you really wish to put substantial confidence in them, should be "blind scored" by *nonpartisan* judges who don't know whether the work samples they judge were produced by students before or after instruction.

Let's face it: if teachers score their own students' pre- and postinstruction work samples, those teachers will naturally want to see improvements as a consequence of their instruction. Teachers are only human, and all humans want to be successful. Accordingly, sometimes subconsciously, teachers will frequently enhance the perceived quality of their students' postinstruction work samples. When evaluating the quality of a specific school, blind scoring by nonpartisans is necessary if one wants to place much confidence in the significance of students' work samples.

Finally, the weight given to work samples in evaluating a school's quality should be based on the significance of the skill (or body of knowledge) represented by those work samples. Suppose a group of middle school's teachers had assembled a substantial amount of pretest-to-posttest work sample evidence of students' writing abilities, all of those work samples having been blind scored by a group of trained, nonpartisan parents and other noneducator citizens. Suppose further that, once the mixed together and undated work samples had been separated (on the basis of previously affixed codes), the contrast between students' pretest and posttest samples indicated that striking gains in students' achievement had taken place. But suppose, finally, that the work samples for these middle school students had only required a student to "write a simple sentence!" What a lot of trouble to go through for such a trifling skill! To be genuinely persuasive, work sample evidence ought to reflect students' attainment of really worthwhile curricular skills.

I should note in passing that, because the collection and scoring of work samples involves a fair amount of effort, almost all real-world work samples that I've run into attempt to measure students' skills, not knowledge. Students' knowledge—that is, memorized facts and information—can usually be assessed more efficiently with less complex assessment approaches such as multiple-choice tests. So while it is possible to measure students' mastery of bodies of knowledge with work sample sorts of tests (often referred to as "performance tests"), it really makes more sense to assess students' mastery of knowledge with less complicated kinds of assessments, such as multiple-choice and true/false tests.

Especially because the use of a pretest-versus-posttest approach allows work samples to mirror the school-year progress (or lack thereof) for students, this evidence source has much to commend it. Yet, everything really depends on what those work samples are and how they were collected and scored. It's also true, of course, that students can get better at performing a skill simply because they get older. Therefore, when pretest-to-posttest evidence is being trotted out, especially for younger students, the gains we see ought to be substantial enough to exceed what might be expected merely because of students' increased maturity.

NONTEST INDICATORS

Even if there were no NCLB in existence, there are sources of evidence, other than students' test performances, that could (and should) be used to evaluate a school's quality. But, of course, there *is* NCLB, and that law specifically stipulates that when a school's or district's adequate yearly progress (AYP) status is determined, "other academic indicators" must be used to do so.

For high schools, NCLB requires that, in addition to students' performances on statewide achievement tests, graduation rates must be used as an academic indicator. A state must signify what levels of graduation rates for its high schools are to be considered acceptable or unacceptable for purposes of AYP. Then the graduation rate for a given high school, or for the high schools in a district, must be contrasted with the state-set minimum graduation rate that has been established in accord with NCLB. A state may also choose to use additional academic indicators for determination of its high school's AYP if it wishes to do so.

Elementary and middle schools must also employ at least one additional academic indicator (beyond students' scores on NCLB-required state tests). However, the law allows a state to identify which academic indicator is to be used in determining the AYP status of schools at these two levels. The regulations for NCLB identify such possibilities as (1) grade-to-grade retention rates; (2) attendance rates; and (3) percentages of students' completing gifted and talented courses. However, states are free to use other academic indicators as long as those indicators clearly bear on determining the effectiveness of a school or a district.

States may, but are not required to, increase the goals for its "other academic indicators" over time. For example, let's assume that student tardiness had been chosen as an additional academic AYP indicator for a state's elementary schools. A state could identify a maximum (acceptable) percentage level of tardiness for an elementary school's students, then decrease that maximum percentage by one percent every other year. In this way, the state's elementary schools would need to systematically reduce student tardiness over an extended time period.

Clearly, the evaluative weight that should be assigned to any non-academic indicator ought to be directly linked to the educational significance of that particular indicator. However, just as important is the defensibility of the expectation levels set for that indicator. Where I now live, in the state of Hawaii, for example, the state's educational officials decided to choose attendance as an additional indicator and decided to set a 95 percent minimum attendance rate to determine AYP for its Elementary and Secondary Education Act Title I schools. If schools failed to achieve a 95 percent attendance rate each year, they were judged to have failed their AYP targets. For a good many schools, of course, a 95 percent attendance rate represents a remarkably demanding requirement. In quite a few schools, both nationally and in Hawaii, typical attendance rates are much lower. So, in Hawaii, even some Title I schools whose students had performed rather well on nationally standardized tests turned out to be

AYP "losers" because, on an academic indicator that is clearly relevant to a school staff's quality, an indefensible expectation level had been set.

Thus, in determining the weight that ought to be assigned to any nontest academic indicator, one needs to consider both the significance of the indicator(s) chosen and the expectation levels assigned to the indicator(s). In judging the quality of a particular school, if one or more nontest indicators have been chosen for determining the school's AYP, be sure to consider the soundness of any such indicator and the defensibility of the state-set expectation linked to that indicator.

In additional, for any state-determined academic indicator, NCLB requires that the state *disaggregate* the data for each school and school district in the same way that you saw in chapter 2, namely, on the basis of race/ethnicity, economically disadvantaged students, students with disabilities, and students with limited English proficiencies. If even one of these subgroups in a particular school fails to attain the state-set level on any state-chosen academic indicator, that school will have failed AYP.

Thus, for each additional nontest academic indicator that a state chooses to incorporate in its AYP calculations, odds rise appreciably that schools or districts will find themselves on the failing end of their annual AYP determinations. To me, it seems unlikely that many states will choose to increase the probable AYP failure rate of the state's schools by adding any nontest indicators beyond the one required by NCLB.

EVIDENCE SOURCES WORKING IN CONCERT—SOMETIMES DISHARMONIOUSLY

The four sources of evidence described in this book can, if employed well, contribute to a defensible judgment about a specific school's effectiveness. But, at bottom, it is still an evaluative judgment. You need to keep in mind that, especially given what you now know about the imprecision of educational tests, even *excellent* educational tests, judgments about school quality are often apt to be wrong. To arrive at the most accurate judgment about a given school's quality, you must look at the categories of evaluative evidence that are at hand, and the caliber of such evidence. If you consider both the significance and the defensibility of any available evidence, you'll probably come up with the best judgment you are apt to make about a specific school's quality. Or, instead, you'll realize that the available evidence, based on its significance and defensibility, just doesn't permit an accurate judgment about a school's effectiveness.

Sometimes reaching a judgment about a particular school's quality is easy. Almost all of the evidence is positive—or, in contrast, almost all of the evidence is negative. Those sorts of evaluative tasks are relatively simple. Unfortunately, they are also far less common than we might wish.

More often than not, the evidence sources for appraising a school will not be in accord. And what that means, of course, is that some serious evidence sifting is required. Certain data sources will have to be given greater weight than others. Sometimes difficult decisions will need to be made, whereby one category of evidence is given importance while another category of evidence is discounted. The real world of school evaluation is fraught with uncertainties and the ever-present potential for error.

If, by this time, you have arrived at a conclusion that there's no unmistakable way to accurately determine a school's quality, you have definitely reached the proper destination. Unfortunately, in most cases there is simply no accuracy-assured procedure for determining whether a particular school is effective or ineffective. Although NCLB sets forth a federally devised framework for designating whether a school is failing or not, the NCLB framework does not ensure fault-free judgments about school failure.

What I want you to recognize is that, because of NCLB, many of America's public schools will be identified as having failed AYP, and as a result may be widely regarded as failing in general. Depending on how many consecutive years they've failed to reach their AYP targets, those schools are to be designated as "on improvement," "in corrective action," or "restructuring." You need to realize that, depending almost totally on how a state has implemented NCLB, many of those "failing" labels will be inaccurate. And, just as serious, some schools that have escaped an AYP-based "failing" label may, in fact, be delivering a less than lustrous education to their students.

Although the evaluation of a particular school may have been made in accord with a set of federal requirements, that evaluation is not necessarily accurate. So if you are a parent of a school age youngster, what you'll need to do is arrive at a personal judgment about the quality of your child's school. Depending on that judgment, you'll then need to decide what action (if any) you ought to take. Similarly, if you are a teacher, and your school's effectiveness has been labeled according to NCLB guidelines, you'll also need to make a personal judgment about the actual quality of your school. And, as was true with parents, you'll need to decide whether any action on your part is warranted.

THE SELF-TEST EXERCISE

To give you some practice in how you might evaluate a particular school's quality, I'm now going to present to you three brief descriptions of absolutely fictitious schools. In the first two of these practice exercises, I'll describe some evaluative evidence regarding a school for which parents have been notified that "the school has failed its AYP target for at least two consecutive years." As a result, official notices have been distributed indicating that—at the district's expense for transportation costs—parents may transfer their child to another district school that has not failed its AYP targets. The most immediate decision facing the parents in each of these first two exercises is whether to transfer their child to another school in the district.

For the third practice exercise, I'll describe a school that has *not* been identified as having failed its AYP targets. In that sort of situation, if a parent has a child in the school that's being described, the parent's most likely choices will typically be to (1) assume the school is doing a reasonably good job, and thus take no action, or (2) contact the school's administrators regarding the quality of the school's instructional program.

At each exercise's conclusion please pause for just a moment to think about what you would do if you were a parent of a child attending the fictitious school just described. Then, after you've made up your own mind, you might want to look at what I think, which will be called Jim's Judgment. It will be presented in boxed italics immediately after the description of evidence regarding a school's quality. You may not agree with me, of course. These postexercise italicized judgments are not, of course, a genuine "answer key." However, with apologies, they're the closest thing to an answer key that I can supply.

If you were, hypothetically, a teacher in any of the three schools described in the practice exercises, you might try to respond as a "pretend parent."

Practice Exercise No. 1: Rhoda Street Elementary School

In the state where Rhoda Street Elementary School is located, the annual NCLB tests administered to all students each spring are the Stanford Achievement Tests–9 (SAT–9). Students' scores in grades three through six of this school for the past two years have improved, but only slightly. Each year, the administration in the month of May of the SAT–9 has shown an overall improvement, but only a slight one. Barely 1 percent more students are being classified annually as "proficient" or "advanced" according to the state's NCLB-required academic achievement levels. The state-set minimum for increased percentages of "proficient-or-better" students each year is actually 4 percent. Failure to achieve this level of improvement has been seen for the school's students overall and for several of the school's disaggregated subgroups—that is, several of those student subgroups with sufficiently large numbers of students.

In early September, and again in mid-May, Rhoda Street Elementary School students in grades two through six completed performance tests calling for students to read a grade-appropriate story, write a brief but well-constructed essay identifying the theme of the story and, having done so, then justify that theme by citing supportive evidence in the story. Students' September and May essays were secretly coded, mixed together, then blind scored by thirteen parent volunteers. After the students' essays had been scored, the essays were re-sorted into pre- and postinstruction essays. Results indicate that almost all of the essays judged to be superior had been written in May—in other words, after teachers' yearlong instructional efforts to promote this combined reading/writing skill.

Attendance at Rhoda Street Elementary has always been excellent. Daily student attendance rates for the past two years at the school have, respectively, been 94 percent and 95 percent. Attendance, incidentally, is a state-designated factor for determining an elementary school's AYP according to NCLB. The school's attendance rates, both overall and for all NCLB-designated subgroups, have always exceeded the state-set 80 percent minimum level in recent years.

Finally, the staff at Rhoda Street Elementary School has been routinely administering anonymous self-reported affective inventories to students on three occasions each year—that is, near the beginning, middle, and end of the school year. These grade-appropriate affective inventories, to be filled out by students who may use only checkmarks, are always administered

and collected with great attention to the preservation of students' anonymity. The affective variables that were dealt with for the past three years
in these ten-item inventories have been (1) students' enjoyment of school,
(2) students' confidence in their ability to read competently, and (3) students' sense that their school is a safe place for them to learn. For each of
the last three years, there have been steady improvements in students'
affect regarding all three of these variables. The increases in students'
enjoyment of school, in fact, have been quite striking.

Because Rhoda Street Elementary School has failed its AYP targets for
two years in a row, its students' parents can now transfer their children
to another district school (one that has not failed AYP).

Now, please think about this situation for a moment. If *you* had a child
in this school, what would *you* do—and why?

Jim's Judgment

*Based on the evidence presented here, if I had a child enrolled in this school,
I would conclude that Rhoda Street Elementary School is doing a pretty good
job despite the "failing" label. The state's selection of a nationally standardized test has set up the school's teachers for near-certain failure. That's
because of the insensitivity of such tests to instruction, even to the detection
of superb instruction. Therefore, I'd totally discount the negative standardized
test data. In contrast, I'd be quite impressed with the other very positive evidence regarding the school's effectiveness. The work samples, dealing with
important reading and writing outcomes, seem to have been properly evaluated. And those work samples show that the school's teachers are doing a
good job in promoting students' reading and writing skills. The affective self-
report evidence, positive as well, appears to have been properly collected.
Kids seem to be enjoying the education provided by the school's teachers.
And the attendance levels are very good indeed. It's not surprising that children who enjoy going to a particular school will attend it regularly. There is, in
short, one type of negative evidence (based on inappropriate tests) counter-
balanced by three solid sorts of positive evidence.*

*If I had a kid in Rhoda Street Elementary School this year, that kid would
be in the same school again next year. I'd conclude that the school's "failing"
label was undeserved.*

Practice Exercise No. 2: Jefferson Elementary School

Jefferson Elementary School is located in a fairly affluent suburban district whose schools, through the years, have been regarded as highly successful because the district's students have historically scored well on the nationally standardized achievement tests the district administers each spring to all students enrolled in grades three through nine.

Two years ago, however, state officials announced that to satisfy the assessment requirements of NCLB, all districts would need to administer newly developed standards-based tests each spring in mathematics and reading. These state-developed tests were designed to assess the most important of the state's curricular aims—that is, the state's content standards for math and reading. Five content standards in mathematics and four content standards in reading were measured by the new tests at each grade level. These nine content standards, all regarded by the state superintendent as "highly significant," have been sufficiently well described so that the state's teachers appear to understand the nature of what is to be assessed. Moreover, students' results are reported on a standard-by-standard basis, thereby informing teachers, students, and students' parents about children's status regarding each assessed standard. In general, the new standards-based tests have been greeted with considerable enthusiasm by the state's educators.

Unfortunately, the students at Jefferson Elementary School have been scoring much lower on the state's new NCLB tests than the students had scored on the previously administered nationally standardized achievement tests. (Incidentally, when the state's new standards-based tests were introduced, district officials decided to abandon administration of the nationally standardized tests in the belief that the district's students would be overtested). For the past two years, the school's students have not scored well on the state's new standards-based tests. Thus, Jefferson Elementary School has been identified as having failed AYP for two consecutive years. That failure was based on the school's inability to reach its statewide AYP target—namely, increasing the school's proportion of proficient-or-better students by at least 5 percent each year. AYP failure was seen in both math and reading. In fact, the students at Jefferson Elementary School earned the lowest scores in reading of the district's nine elementary schools. Only one other district school failed to make its AYP targets, and that deficit was seen only in mathematics.

The school's attendance rates, however, were exceedingly high. The average daily attendance levels for the past two school years at Jefferson Elementary were, respectively, 95.1 percent and 94.8 percent Attendance had been identified as an additional NCLB-required academic indicator by state officials—with a required minimum average attendance rate per school of 87 percent. The school's incidence of tardiness (required by the district, but not by the state, for inclusion in all reports to parents) was exceedingly low. On average, the level of student tardiness at Jefferson Elementary School was less than 1 percent per day.

The teachers at Jefferson Elementary School have traditionally provided parents with end-of-year "showcase portfolios" of students' best work (in writing, mathematics, and social studies) at the final "parents-at-school" night of the school year. As usual, in both of the past two years, students' end-of-year portfolios contained many examples of high-quality student work.

Because all parents of students in Jefferson Elementary School have been offered the choice of having their child transfer to another "non-failing" school in the district, those parents now must make a decision.

Suppose *you* were one of those parents, and *you* had a fourth-grade child in Jefferson Elementary School. Pause for a moment, think about the evidence just presented, then decide what *your* decision would be. And why would you make that decision?

Jim's Judgment

If my fourth grader were enrolled in Jefferson Elementary School, I would believe in the accuracy of the "failing" label given to the school. The chief reason for my belief is that the state's new NCLB standards-based tests seem to be pretty good ones, and the school's students are stumbling badly on those tests. In the past, of course, Jefferson Elementary School students have done well on nationally standardized achievement tests. But students' performances on such tests are often influenced dramatically by the socioeconomic backgrounds of students' families. And—let's face it—most of the children attending Jefferson Elementary come from rather affluent homes. Students' scores on those previously administered national achievement tests may have been a function of what the school's students brought to school rather than what they were taught at school.

> Other than the positive attendance and tardiness data, there is no other evidence to contradict the school's less-than-desired student test performances in both reading and mathematics. And it's important to note that other elementary schools in the district are doing quite well in getting more students to score at a "proficient" level on the state's new tests. The weak performance of Jefferson Elementary students on a test that measures a modest number of significant skills is, to me, particularly troubling.
>
> I'd definitely shop for a better school for my child. Jefferson's teachers don't seem to be promoting students' satisfactory growth. Some children, it appears, are being "left behind." I wouldn't want my child to be among them.

Practice Exercise No. 3: Lincoln High School

In the state where Lincoln High School is located, the tests selected for implementation of NCLB are standards-based tests developed by one of the testing companies that routinely creates nationally standardized achievement tests. The company was able to employ many of its off-the-shelf items to construct a series of tests that its executive vice president regards as "reasonably well aligned" with the state's officially approved content standards (thirty-seven content standards in reading and ninety-two content standards in mathematics). The correlations between students' scores on these newly created standards-based tests and students' scores on nationally standardized achievement tests are quite high, thus indicating that the national achievement tests and the state's new standards-based achievement tests tend to measure the same sorts of things.

Lincoln High School is in a metropolitan school district, but has few minority students because the school is located in the center of a large middle-class (mostly upper-middle-class) section of the district.

Because Lincoln's students have performed well on the state's new NCLB tests for the past two years, the school has not failed to meet its AYP targets in either reading or mathematics. And, because there are insufficient numbers of enrolled students representing each of the NCLB-stipulated subgroups whose performances must be disaggregated, Lincoln High School's annual AYP performance has also been satisfactory with respect to subgroup disaggregations. (There were, in fact, no subgroups to be disaggregated.) The only other state-specified NCLB academic indicator is the one set by federal law—namely, graduation rate. Lincoln High has routinely been graduating sufficient numbers of its students to more than exceed the state-set minimum graduation requirement that 75 percent of a high school's students be graduated.

There is no other evaluative information regarding school quality available in the district's "Annual Report To Parents Regarding Your Child's High School." If parents wish to learn more about this school's effectiveness, they are urged to confer with the school's principal or either of its two assistant principals.

Now, assume that your child is enrolled as a tenth grader in Lincoln High. Do you conclude that the teachers at the school are doing a satisfactory job? Pause for a moment and think about the evidence available for Lincoln High. Based on the absence of a "failing school" report card, should *you* assume that the instruction at your child's high school is effective? If not, what might *you* do about it?

Jim's Judgment

The situation at Lincoln High is a common one, especially apt to be encountered in settings where NCLB tests have been adopted that are strongly linked to students' socioeconomic status (SES). And the test being used for NCLB in this instance, even though it is called a standards-based test, appears to be strongly influenced by students' SES. All nationally standardized tests are definitely SES-related. This state's NCLB test also appears to be linked to children's SES, quite possibly because a major test-development firm used many of its off-the-shelf items (from the firm's achievement exams) to create the new state test.

Because that's so, and because there is almost no other credible evidence reflective of the school staff's effectiveness, I would be far from tranquil about the quality of my child's school. I'm not saying the school's staff is ineffective, because that certainly may not be so. But there's simply no compelling evidence regarding the school's effectiveness—one way or the other.

Accordingly, as a parent, I'd try to ferret out more information about the school's quality. I'd try to spend time in the school itself, talking with its teachers. I'd certainly want to spend time with my own child to get a student's perception about what's going on at school. Finally, I'd schedule meetings with the school's principal and both of its assistant principals to see if they could provide any additional evidence relevant to the school's quality.

What I'm suggesting is simply this: Because of the apparent use of a state-selected NCLB test that is likely to be instructionally insensitive, the absence of a "failed-AYP" label for a school does not automatically mean that the school is, in fact, successful. For Lincoln High, I'd recommend that parents try to collect more quality-relevant evidence. I know that's what I'd try to do.

LOOKING BACK

As I hope you now see, the determination of a particular school's quality is a challenging enterprise. Even if given the best possible evidence, it is often difficult to arrive at sound judgments about whether a given school is effective or ineffective. But in many settings, the evidence will not be the best that's possible. And the absence of high-quality evidence makes the evaluation of a particular school much tougher, if not impossible.

Because NCLB presents a series of important choices to the parents of children whose schools have flopped on one or more state-set AYP requirements, it is especially important for such parents to determine whether their child's school is "failing" in name only or, in contrast, is truly a *failing*—without quotation marks—school.

What I hope you've recognized by now is that any judgments regarding the quality of a school should be dependent on the amount and caliber of the available evidence relevant to that school's effectiveness. It will be foolish for parents to automatically assume that their children's "failing" school is so bad that instant flight to another school in the district is warranted. Such parents may be taking their children from one frying pan and simply placing them in another, possibly more geographically distant, frying pan.

If a given state's educational policy makers have chosen suitable NCLB tests to determine their schools' AYP, and have selected significant nontest academic indicators to bolster AYP decisions, then parents can typically trust the meaningfulness of labels given to "AYP failing" schools. If such is not the case, especially if the state's NCLB tests are not instructionally sensitive, then a school that has been labeled as failing may not be. Just as a jury needs sufficient evidence to find any defendant guilty or innocent, parents and teachers need sufficient evidence to decide if a child's school is truly failing. Some labels, even federally authorized labels, are false.

Conclusion
What To Do Now?

This chapter will be of greatest interest to those who have an interest in *doing something* about the way our schools are being evaluated. Doing something, of course, doesn't necessarily mean that you need to change anything. If your state's implementation of NCLB is defensible, then doing something might simply translate into your sending a letter of appreciation to the education officials in your state. On the other hand, if your state's policy makers have implemented NCLB in an inappropriate manner, then doing something might involve your engaging in activities that could help modify the way your state's schools are being evaluated. It's up to you.

FOR EDUCATORS, PARENTS, AND CONCERNED CITIZENS

Because each state, according to the provisions of NCLB, is allowed to implement this federal law largely in its own way, there will surely be state-to-state differences in the way that state officials choose to install the school evaluation programs called for in NCLB. Even though this federal law contains some heavy-duty constraints about the nature of the components in any state's accountability-focused system of school evaluation, each state can make many key implementation decisions. Those decisions will result in the state's NCLB-based evaluations of schools having either a positive or a negative effect on the state's public schools. For example, I have stressed and restressed that a state's selection of the NCLB achievement tests used to collect adequate yearly progress (AYP) data will cause schools to be regarded as champs or chumps. Appropriate achievement tests give a state's school evaluation system a chance to be beneficial; inappropriate achievement tests will almost certainly cause the state's school evaluation program to cause educational harm.

What I'm going to be recommending here is basically a two-step approach. In Step 1 you'll need to understand the fundamentals of how your state's NCLB-based school accountability system works. Then, as Step 2, if the system is defensible, you need to decide what, if anything, you need to do about that benign situation. Or, if that system is not defensible, you need to decide what, if anything, you're going to do about that harmful situation.

Understanding Your State's NCLB Accountability System

The first thing concerned individuals need to do is find out what's going on in their state regarding implementation of NCLB's accountability requirements. Because educators are likely to be more familiar with whom to contact in order to secure such information, they can usually identify the individual(s) who can supply NCLB-related information. Typically, such information can be secured from state department personnel or, in larger school districts, from district-level staff.

You might also try contacting your state's chief state school officer—typically, your state superintendent of schools or state commissioner of schools—and raising questions about the most significant of the state's key NCLB decisions. Or you might also address such questions to one or more members of your state's school board. (Names and addresses of your state's superintendent or its school board members can usually be secured by a letter or a phone call to your state's department of education. State departments of education, by the way, may be described in certain states by other names, such as the Office of the Superintendent of Public Instruction.) You might inquire, in a letter or via e-mail, regarding answers to several of the following questions.

State Tests

- What tests are used in our state to satisfy the provisions of NCLB?
- Are these tests instructionally supportive? That is, do they help our state's teachers in their efforts to promote students' progress?
- Are our state's NCLB tests accompanied by genuinely clear descriptions of the content standards they are intended to assess?
- How many content standards do our state's NCLB tests attempt to assess?
- Do the tests, each year, measure students' mastery of our state's most significant content standards?
- Are teachers and parents provided with students' results so it is possible to determine which content standards have/haven't been mastered by a student?

Adequate Yearly Progress

- What increase is required each year in the proportion of a school's students who must score at a proficient-or-above level on our state's NCLB-required tests?
- What procedures were used to establish these required annual increases?
- Who participated in the decisions to establish these minimum required levels of adequate yearly progress?
- What is the minimum number of students required in our state for the scores of a subgroup (for example, a school's African American students) to be incorporated in the school's annual AYP determinations?
- Does our state use confidence intervals to identify schools that have failed to reach their AYP targets?

Academic Achievement Standards

- What are our state's academic achievement standards? That is, what levels of student test performance are required for each identified level of student achievement such as "basic" or "proficient"?
- How were the levels for our state's NCLB-required academic achievement (content) standards established?
- Who participated in the determination of our state's academic achievement (content) standards?

Other Academic Indicators

- What nontest indicators are to be used in determining adequate yearly progress for students in our state's elementary, middle, and high schools?
- Who selected those nontest indicators of a school's success?
- What are the state-set AYP expectation levels for each of these other academic indicators?

Let's say that you decided to use questions such as these, or that instead you came up with your own questions along these lines. If you get answers from your state's superintendent, members of your state's school board, or other sources, you'll then be in a position to reach a decision regarding whether you believe your state's implementation of NCLB is reasonable. If it is, then you can accept your state's school evaluation system. If it isn't reasonable, then don't accept it.

Typically, you'll need to think back a bit to the kinds of issues described in earlier chapters so you can decide whether your state's implementation of NCLB's school evaluation requirements seems likely to benefit or erode educational quality in your state. For instance, if you discover that traditionally constructed standardized achievement tests have been adopted as your state's NCLB tests—tests that focus on comparative interpretations—then you can be pretty sure your state's tests will be instructionally insensitive. Those tests just aren't able to do an accurate job of producing meaningful school-specific evaluative data. And, as a result, it's almost certain that a number of harmful instructional practices will be taking place in the state's classrooms. Your state's teachers will be pressured to improve their students' scores on tests that were never intended to detect instructional improvement.

Similarly, you might find out that a set of newly developed standards-based tests is being used for your state's NCLB school evaluations. However, you discover that those new tests are supposed to measure students' mastery of so many state-approved content standards that (1) not all of the state's content standards can ever be measured by a given year's test and (2) there are so few items measuring each content standard (the ones that are actually assessed) that no instructionally helpful results are provided to teachers, students, or parents. Because such mushy tests are also instructionally insensitive, and thus will contribute to inaccurate school evaluations, those tests will lead to a deterioration in the quality of education seen in your state's schools.

For teachers who discover that their state is employing instructionally insensitive NCLB tests it may be that you will not be engaging in unsuitable classroom activities just because of those tests. However, it is almost certain that a fair number of your colleagues might. As an educator, you need to worry about what's going on instructionally all across your state, not just in your classroom.

You might learn, however, that your state has established some genuinely challenging, yet attainable levels of student performance for its NCLB-required academic achievement standards. You might also discover that, at every important point in the creation of your state's NCLB-required approach to school evaluation, representatives from all key stakeholders have been involved—that is, teachers, parents, and even students—and that sensible expectations for schools' performances appear to have been set.

You might find out that officials in your state have really tried to create a set of instructionally supportive achievement tests that attempt to measure only a handful of supersignificant student skills. Moreover, teachers are being informed about what's to be measured each year and, after the tests have been administered, teachers and parents find out how students have performed on each content standard (or benchmark) that these NCLB tests measure.

Whatever the case, clearly some aspects of your state's NCLB-based evaluation of schools may make educational sense; others may not. You need to figure out which parts constitute sound elements of the accountability system and which parts are unsound, then make a judgment regarding the overall defensibility of the state's entire NCLB school evaluation program.

A Defensible State Implementation

Let's assume that you've collected a fair amount of information about the workings of your state's NCLB-based accountability program for evaluating schools. Will you ever be able to conclude for certain that the state's evaluative program is a good one or a bad one? Probably not. These sorts of evaluative enterprises are genuinely complicated, and it is difficult for individuals—even reasonably assertive ones—to collect sufficient information to make a definitive judgment about the defensibility of your state's school evaluation procedures.

For illustrative purposes, however, suppose you have obtained information that makes you feel pretty positive about your state's public-school accountability program. For example, you might have learned that the state's school evaluation system is organized around a relatively small number of genuinely challenging academic content standards in reading and mathematics—standards such as a child's ability to read, with non-superficial comprehension, various kinds of written materials. Moreover, you find out that new, custom-developed achievement tests are to be used to measure each student's mastery of these challenging content standards. Those achievement tests will provide standard-by-standard reports to teachers, students, and students' parents. And, because the new state NCLB tests are also accompanied by clear descriptions of each content standard being assessed, the state's teachers seem to understand the essence of the content standards being assessed. Finally, what seems to be a sensible set of nontest indicators (such as attendance levels and grade-to-grade promotion rates) have been incorporated into each year's determination of a school's success in meeting its NCLB-imposed AYP targets.

Assume, if you're an educator, that you've had an opportunity to speak with a number of your colleagues who appear to be conversant with the chief features of your state's NCLB accountability system. Although those colleagues are, without exception, apprehensive about how long they can continue to promote the annually required increases (in the number of students scoring at a proficient-or-better level on the state's new tests), they generally regard the state's accountability system as both fair and accurate. If you are a "noneducator" citizen, let's assume you've talked with a substantial collection of public school teachers and administrators who, in general, approve of the state's NCLB-based accountability system. Given the information you have at hand, you might reasonably conclude that your state's NCLB-based accountability system is defensible. What, then, is the point?

My suggestion is that you try to contribute to public support and educator support of the NCLB-based accountability system in your state. It appears to be a system in which "failing" schools are *truly failing* and, just as important, schools that haven't been identified as failing probably aren't. You must recognize that there will be many people who'll be criticizing the accountability system—particularly those educators working in schools that have missed the mark in meeting their school's AYP targets or the parents of children who attend those schools. If the state's system seems to be a good one, however, you need to register your view that it appears to be a defensible school evaluation operation—even though some folks won't agree with you. Your focus must be on what's best for the state's children, and not what most pleases adults.

To demonstrate your support you might send a letter of commendation to your state's education authorities—for instance, to the state superintendent of schools or to members of the state school board. You could also send a letter to the editor of one or more local newspapers suggesting that your personal analysis of the state's NCLB school accountability program is a sensible one. Similar opinions could also be voiced on local radio or TV talk shows. In sum, you can do whatever your energy level permits to let the world know that, in your view, the state's way of appraising its schools is well grounded.

An Indefensible State Implementation

To be honest, however, I fear that it's more likely that the wrong sorts of statewide achievement tests will often have been selected, frequently because of assessment naïveté on the part of a state's key educational policy makers. As a consequence, the state's system for evaluating its public school educators may be based on instructionally insensitive tests that fail to give those educators a fair opportunity to demonstrate just how effective they really are. Due to the tremendous score-boosting pressures placed on the state's teachers, a number of unsound classroom instructional practices will usually follow. And, because of those serious instructional shortcomings in the state's classrooms, many of the state's students will receive a far worse education than they would otherwise be receiving.

What do you do if you conclude that, in all likelihood, your state's school evaluation accountability program is seriously flawed? Well, for openers, you try to get the program fixed.

I suggest that—with far more fervor than was warranted if the state's accountability program had turned out to be defensible—you get the word out, and especially to the state's educational policy makers. Let them know that, in your opinion, there is a profound need to improve the state's school accountability program.

You could communicate—by letter, telephone, e-mail, or in person—with key educational decision makers in your state. A state school board is a good place to start. This is also a wonderful opportunity to let your state's elected legislators know that there may be an important, federally funded accountability program in their state—a program likely to harm—not help—the state's students. Letters to the editor, listserv groups, radio talk shows, and so on—all of these efforts can help. You need to make it plain that you are not opposed to school-focused accountability programs. What you want to do is isolate the specific weaknesses in the state's NCLB-based school evaluation program, then suggest how those weaknesses might be remedied.

If your state's school evaluation system is truly injurious, you'll find that many of your state's educators will also be outraged by it. Similarly, many parents of school-age children will surely be dismayed by what they regard as an improper method of appraising their children's teachers. The worse your state's educational accountability system is, the more allies there will be out there just waiting for you to find. These folks will usually welcome the chance to work in collaboration with you.

Educators who criticize the system are going to be saddled with a tough handicap—namely, perceived partisanship. Because educators who argue against NCLB-based school evaluations will often be viewed as individuals who are unwilling to be held accountable, you really need to stimulate interest in this issue on the part of those individuals who are patently nonpartisan. Parent groups and business roundtables invariably end up with more political clout than educator groups, even though educators' appraisal of the state's school evaluation system may be wholly accurate. Parents and members of the business community, once apprised of this situation, will almost always end up being more influential than educators can be. If you're a dissatisfied educator, get such noneducators interested in these issues, then *disaffiliate*, leaving them to act in their own, nonpartisan ways.

But let's be realistic. It will be tough to modify or replace a state-level NCLB school evaluation system that is already in place. Many people will have contributed to that system's creation, and many dollars will have been spent to get it up and running. So if you find that your state's NCLB accountability system is not likely to be meaningfully altered, then your next best step is to promote a substantial *assessment literacy* education campaign.

Attempt to educate others regarding the reasons that their state's school accountability program appears to be flawed. You might refer them to this book or to others I've listed following this chapter. What you must try to do is promote a more knowledgeable group of individuals in your state. The state's evaluation program has the potential to influence your state's classroom activities in either positive or negative ways. A more assessment-literate public is apt to recognize when the wrong tests are being used for a task that is unarguably important—namely, judging the quality of a state's public schools.

FOR PARENTS OF SCHOOL-AGE CHILDREN

What is most important for parents of school-age children to find out is whether an evaluation of a particular school is likely to be accurate. Then, depending on that accuracy, parents will need to decide what, if anything, to do about it. And what to do, of course, depends on whether the evaluation of the school was positive or negative. The first step, again, is to find out about your state's school evaluation procedures and, then, take appropriate action based on the specific evaluation of your child's school.

Understanding How Your Child's School Was Evaluated

Much of this book has described the ways in which schools can be accurately and inaccurately evaluated. If you've received an annual report card from your school district evaluating your child's school, you need to determine whether that evaluation is most likely correct or incorrect. To make such a determination, you need to get a good fix on the chief factors that led to the evaluation, and one of the most direct ways of getting the information you need is to make an appointment with the principal of your child's school. When you call to set up such an appointment, indicate that your chief purpose is to learn more about the process being used—in your state and, specifically, in your district—to evaluate schools.

First you must recognize that your school's principal may not have all the information you'll need. While school principals are supposed to be the instructional leaders of their schools, it's definitely possible that an already busy principal may not know enough about the NCLB-based school evaluation process in your state. You may need to seek additional information from school district officials or even from personnel in your state department of education. However, to make my suggestions easier to deal with, I'm going to assume that your school's principal understands the state's school evaluation system well enough that you'll get direct answers to most questions about school evaluation that you might ask. If I were you, I'd be tossing many of the following questions at the principal:

NCLB-Required Tests

- What tests are being given to students in our school to satisfy the assessment requirements of NCLB?
- Recognizing that these tests were chosen by state officials, not you, what is your personal opinion about whether students' scores on these tests accurately reflect the instructional effectiveness of the teachers in this school?
- Do you think the teachers in our school have a very clear idea about the skills and/or knowledge being assessed by these tests? That is, do they have a sufficiently clear idea for their classroom instructional planning purposes?
- How many content standards are assessed each year by our state's NCLB tests?
- Can you show me examples of any state-issued descriptive information that our school's teachers can draw on to help them determine what is going to be tested each year by these state-required tests?
- Do our school's teachers receive reports of test results that indicate which assessed curricular aims have or haven't been mastered by each child who has been tested?

Adequate Yearly Progress

- Does our state's AYP timeline call for single-year or multiyear increments and, if multiyear increments are involved, where do they occur in the timeline?
- What annual state-determined increases (per increment) are required in the percent of our school's students who must be identified as "proficient or above"?
- What percent of our school's students are currently scoring at proficient-or-above levels on the state's NCLB-required tests?

- What is your prediction for future years with respect to the percentages of students who will be scoring at a proficient-or-above level in our school?
- What is the state-set minimum number of students needed so that an NCLB-designated subgroup (for example, Hispanic Americans) will be incorporated in our school's annual AYP determinations?
- How many test scores of NCLB-designated subgroups, if any, are currently being used in the calculation of our school's AYP status?
- Does our state use confidence intervals in the identification of AYP-failing schools?

Academic Achievement Standards

- What are our state's academic achievement standards? For instance, what are the test score performance levels that students in our school must earn in order to be classified at different levels such as "proficient" or "advanced"?
- What percent of our school's students are currently performing at each of these state-specified achievement levels?
- How appropriate do you believe our state's academic achievement standards actually are?

Other Academic Indicators

- What nontest indicators does the state require to be used in determining if our school has attained its AYP targets?
- What minimum levels are required for our school's students to satisfy these other academic indicators?
- What is your personal opinion of the usefulness of these other academic indicators in determining our school's quality?

Overall

- What is your own, overall professional judgment about the NCLB-based process being used in our state to evaluate the state's public schools?
- How accurate do you believe the state-determined evaluation of our school is? Why?

After considering the answers to such questions from the principal of your child's school, together with the kinds of test results we've seen that are (or aren't) useful in appraising a school's quality, you will most likely be in a position to make at least a tentative judgment regarding the accuracy of the NCLB-based evaluation of your child's school.

Suppose the annual report card for your child's school indicated that, because of inadequate AYP, the school had been placed on an "improvement" track. Based on your estimate of the accuracy of the school evaluation process being used, you'd be able to conclude whether that negative appraisal appears to be warranted. Conversely, if the school's annual report card showed that your child's school had made sufficient AYP, and thus was not "failing," you'd be able to decide whether the school is really performing as satisfactorily as it appears to be.

A Positive Evaluation of the School

If the evaluation of your child's school is a positive one, and you've reached a conclusion that the school evaluation approach being used in your state seems sensible, then your child appears to be in a school that can offer a good education. Congratulations!

If, however, you are convinced that the school evaluation model in your state is less than ideal, you can't be complacent about a positively appraised school. Try to dig deeper into the evidence that can help you determine—beyond what NCLB requires—whether your child's school is genuinely effective. Take a look again at the issues raised earlier in this book. See if you can get the school's teachers or administrators to make available to you any additional information such as students' work samples or evidence of students' affect.

The less confidence you have in the state's procedure for evaluating its schools, the more information you'll need to convince you that any positive evaluation of your child's school was really deserved. Talking to the school's administrators and teachers is a great way to come up with additional insights about the school's quality. The more information that you can assemble about the actual quality of an NCLB "nonfailing" school, the more confidence you will have that the school is or isn't doing a good instructional job.

A Negative Evaluation of the School

By far the most troublesome school evaluation situation for parents arises when they receive a report card indicating that their child's school is not performing satisfactorily. Given today's NCLB-generated approach to school evaluation, that negative appraisal of your child's school is almost certain to be based on the school's failure to meet its AYP targets, either for the entire student body or for an NCLB-designated subgroup. The question before you, of course, is: What should you do about it?

First off, you'll need to focus on that "failing" school label in light of your earlier judgment about the accuracy of any of your state's school appraisals. Are those evaluations really based on accurate test data or, instead, are they based on data derived from instructionally insensitive tests? The more doubtful you are about the defensibility of your state's implementation of NCLB's school evaluation regulations, the less confidence you should place in a negative evaluation of your child's school.

If I were you, however, I'd definitely want to do some additional data gathering at the school itself to try to confirm or negate the idea that your child is enrolled in a failing school. Conversations with the school's administrators and teachers can sometimes be especially helpful. Simply asking those educators, in as nonthreatening manner as possible, to comment on the quality of the school will often yield some powerful insights. Ask those educators what evidence is available to confirm their evaluative judgments. Remember, the teachers and administrators of schools that have received "failing" evaluations are understandably apt to be more than a little defensive, so you'll need plenty of tact when trying to find out how accurate a state-based negative appraisal really was. Try, again in a nonthreatening manner, to dig beneath the defensiveness that you're almost certain to encounter.

It's really okay to ask teachers to trot out evidence for you regarding a school's effectiveness—or lack of it. What you need, and what you have a right to expect, is something more solid than a collection of teachers' self-interested "everything's great" comments. You're looking for facts—that is, for evidence—that you can rely on to help you judge the quality of your child' school.

The School Transfer Decision

After a school has failed to attain its AYP targets for two consecutive years, you'll typically be given the opportunity to transfer your child to another "nonfailing" school in the district. That's a major decision, of course, and it requires plenty of careful thinking.

If you conclude that the appraisal of your child's school is based on a pretty shaky foundation, then I recommend that you not take any transfer action. Moreover, if the state's system of school evaluation is flawed, how can you be sure that the new school to which your child is transferred will be all that great? Remember, if your state's school evaluation system seems shoddy, then not only may the "failing" label that's been laid on your child's school be inaccurate; so too may be the "nonfailing" labels affixed to the other schools in the district.

NCLB requires that the district pick up transportation costs (from its federally supplied dollars) when transferring students from schools receiving Elementary and Secondary Education Act (ESEA) funds. However, the transferring of children to different schools involves much more than "Who pays for the bus ride?" There's likely to be plenty of personal distress involved, particularly for younger children. Their school friends will often be difficult to replace. Because your child is probably now enrolled in a school that's close to your home, how desirable or safe is it to have the child bussed farther away from your home?

Those who believe it is obvious that a child attending a failing school must be instantly transferred to a nonfailing school just aren't thinking about all the practical realities involved. When parents of children attending ESEA Title I schools who had failed AYP for two years in the state where I live were informed in 2002 that they could transfer their children to another public school, almost no parents did. My conversations with those parents indicated from them a genuine lack of confidence in the way that the negative appraisals of their children's schools had been reached. (Better the devil you know, than the devil you don't.) And the parents with whom I spoke, especially those who had children in elementary schools, just didn't want those youngsters going to a faraway school. Close to home was, in their view, better.

On the other hand, in some locales there are so many parents who want their children transferred to other, nonfailing schools that those transfers literally overload the system. In New York City, for example, about eight thousand parents wanted their kids to be transferred to nonfailing schools, but those schools received no additional resources to cope with this influx of transfer students. Predictably, the result was educational chaos.

I guess what it comes down to is this: a negatively evaluated school may not really be ineffective. I wish that I could spell out a series of surefire steps that would lead to a definitive evaluation of a school's success. But unless a school is spectacularly stellar or unarguably awful, it is really difficult to make an accurate appraisal of its success. There are many factors that should be considered, and parents typically don't always have access to all the relevant information they need—and sometimes wouldn't know how to interpret it if they had such information.

The passage of NCLB may have made this historically tough task even tougher. The trouble is that many parents will now attach more significance to these federally decreed school appraisals than those appraisals really warrant. As you'll surely know by this point, I've been constantly arguing that the validity of any NCLB-based program for evaluating schools depends completely on the way a state's educational decision makers added flesh to NCLB's legally mandated bones.

A state's NCLB-based accountability system is likely to produce accurate evaluations of state schools if it (1) is organized around a modest number of truly significant reading and math curricular outcomes, (2) incorporates sensible expectations regarding what levels of performance should constitute students' "proficiency," and (3) uses instructionally supportive tests that yield both accurate accountability evidence and also contribute to improved classroom instruction. If you find that such an accountability system is being used in your state, then you can have a fair amount of confidence that some schools judged to be failing really are, in fact, failing. You can also believe that most schools judged to be not failing really are, in fact, not failing.

A state's NCLB-based accountability system is almost certain to produce inaccurate evaluations of state schools if it (1) attempts to assess too many content standards, (2) fails to clearly describe what its NCLB tests are measuring, (3) has established proficiency level expectations that are far too high or far too low, or (4) employs instructionally insensitive NCLB tests. If you live in a state whose NCLB school evaluation system reflects one or more of these serious shortcomings, you should be reluctant to attribute much accuracy at all to any evaluation of your child's school.

To make NCLB really work for the improved education of children, that federal law has to be carried out in an enlightened manner. My guess is that, in well over half of our states, enlightenment in the implementation of NCLB is currently in short supply. Putting it another way, I think that you are more likely to discover your state's NCLB-based school evaluations are flawed than you are to discover that they are fine. But the only way for you to know how much confidence you can place in a "failing" evaluation of a school is to learn more about how your state is carrying out NCLB's accountability provisions. There's simply no other way.

THE PAST AND FUTURE OF NCLB

If you were to review the 1965 version of the ESEA you'd discover that its congressional architects were trying to create a series of federal financial incentives so that economically disadvantaged children, those who often were getting the short end of the education stick, would receive a better education. That was clearly a praiseworthy aspiration. But, even back then, many federal lawmakers were doubtful about whether the federal dollars they were soon going to be dispensing to states would be properly spent at the local level. That is, they were worried about whether the ESEA would really improve the education of those students traditionally underserved by our public schools.

With each successive reauthorization of the ESEA, and especially the alterations to Title I of that law (the heavily funded section of the law focused on disadvantaged students), we have seen the U.S. Congress install additional safeguards to help identify schools that were or were not doing a good educational job for disadvantaged students. But American educators, as is true with any collections of human beings, want to succeed, not fail. Thus, as additional evaluative constraints were appended to each reauthorization of ESEA, many of our nation's education officials figured out ways to dodge federal scrutiny or, more accurately, figured out ways to look good instead of bad.

For example, if required to make AYP, state policy makers often opted for tiny levels of annual required progress. Such trivial levels of improvement, if they occurred at all, were often not attributable to improved instruction, but rather to teachers' familiarity with the tests themselves (and, therefore, teachers' introduction of this year's tested content into next year's lessons). ESEA's adequate yearly progress safeguards were subverted by education officials.

In the past, if students' scores on federally required tests were supposed to provide an indication of how well a school was succeeding in using

ESEA funds to serve its disadvantaged students, then some school administrators would arrange student activities so that those students most likely to score low on a required achievement test would be conveniently "taking a field trip to the state capitol" on the very day that the state's accountability tests were to be administered. Now, however, NCLB says that if at least 95 percent of enrolled students do not complete the state's required achievement tests, a school automatically fails its AYP.

Rarely did we see educational officials, by their own choice, break out the test scores of traditionally underserved student groups such as African Americans, Hispanic Americans, or students with disabilities. The AYP requirements of NCLB now require such disaggregations whenever there are sufficient numbers of students in a school or district. Another loophole has been closed.

As I have noted, education officials are only normal. And normal folks want to be evaluated positively. Over the years, therefore, America's education officials have continually figured out ways to beat the evaluative stipulations generated by earlier versions of the ESEA. But with the enactment of NCLB, the ESEA accountability game's evaluation rules became much tougher to beat.

Given our nation's sorry history of ESEA implementation for more than three decades, the bipartisan lawmakers who designed its most recent reauthorization—that is, NCLB—simply weren't in a mood to be tricked anymore. If you spend much time in pondering the new law's accountability provisions, I think you'll agree that one message comes through in unmistakable terms: "Educators, you need to show us the evidence that not only disadvantaged children, but *all* children, are being well educated!" The law is laden with safeguards, constraints, and monitoring mechanisms. Although NCLB leaves many important decisions to the states, the law also sets forth a series of stringent requirements so that local educators will be less able to dodge the intentions of those who crafted the most recent version of ESEA.

Even so, as you have seen, it is still possible for a state's educational officials to sidestep these fine legislative intentions by employing inventive AYP timelines and all sorts of statistical gimmickry to dodge AYP failure. Unfortunately, one of the specific mechanisms to make sure that all children were well served in the nation's public schools may actually have created the very reason that, in several years, NCLB will *implode*. I am referring specifically to the lofty aspiration that, by the 2013–14 school year, all children, including all members of the many NCLB-designated subgroups, will have earned proficient-or-better scores on a state's standardized academic assessments. That's a marvelous goal. Unfortunately, it's a marvelous goal that's clearly not going to be achieved.

Anyone who spends even a few hours in a few of today's public schools will recognize that teachers will be unable to get every single child in school to reach a meaningful proficiency level on any sort of sensible achievement test. "One hundred percent of children reaching proficiency" has a potent political ring to it, but it is an altogether unrealistic aspiration. What makes more sense, of course, is for educators to set a goal of getting as many students to become proficient as is humanly possible. American educators will need to do a remarkably effective job to accomplish even that more realistic educational goal.

Yet, the politically correct goal of 100 percent proficient students in twelve years has led to a federally required timeline for states whereby substantial and equal increments are required in the proportions of the state's students who become proficient. If a school does not attain its AYP targets (not only for all of its students, but also for all of its legally identified, sufficiently large subgroups), then the school will have failed AYP and will soon be placed on an improvement cycle that may lead to serious sanctions that could result in the school's being closed.

Well, in the first few years after NCLB became a law, a certain proportion of the nation's schools will have sufficient numbers of students who already score high enough on their state's accountability tests so that a considerable group of public schools will be able to meet their AYP targets. Remember, many states will probably end up choosing instructionally insensitive achievement tests for which students' socioeconomic status (SES) turn out to be the most important determiner of students' scores. Thus, in those schools serving upper-level SES families, students' test scores will probably be high enough, early on, to make the state's AYP annual targets. But let's say, for instance, that a state-set AYP improvement rate of 5 percent per year has been established. For a few years there will be a number of schools whose students score sufficiently well on state tests to avoid AYP failure, especially for high-SES schools. But as each year goes by, the number of nonfailing schools will get smaller and smaller. Remember, even in states that have chosen to employ "start slow, finish fast" AYP timelines, meaningful levels of student progress will ultimately be required.

How will parents, educators, and their elected representatives respond when it turns out that, for example, 80 or 90 percent of this nation's public schools are labeled as failing? Complaints from disgruntled parents whose children are attending a failing school will loudly ricochet around state capitals and Washington, D.C. Common sense alone tells us that so many of our nation's public schools just aren't that bad! At such a moment, I predict, our federal lawmakers will be forced to rethink the wisdom of NCLB's "dozen-years-to-proficiency" requirement and will establish more realistic annual improvement goals.

My chief worry, however, is that during the years between now and then, in where unenlightened implementations of NCLB are present, thousands of children will be educationally marred, perhaps permanently, because teachers will have been pressured to accomplish AYP improvement goals that—in truth—are instructionally unaccomplishable.

Some apologists for NCLB have argued that, although many schools will be identified as ineffectual because of the failure to make their annual AYP targets, no serious harm will be done to those schools because there's really not all that much federal money, per school, to be either dispensed or denied. This, however, is subpar thinking. How do you think that teachers will feel about themselves after they have been identified as staff members of a failing school? How do you think that children will feel about their school and themselves after their school is identified as failing? I've personally seen teachers weep after having been (incorrectly) identified as working in a failing school. I've personally talked to students who morosely reported that their school "stinks." The impact of undeserved "failing" labels on both educators and students will, unarguably, be profound. A state that fails to properly install its NCLB accountability system dooms its educators and their students to wear labels that hurt.

In an undisguised attempt to force American educators to improve the quality of their instruction, this latest version of ESEA has set forth a number of achievement aspirations that are altogether unrealistic. Telling educators that all their students must be proficient in a dozen years may make for persuasive political rhetoric, but the establishment of expectations that are unattainable will rarely spur people to perform at new levels of excellence. On the contrary, unrealistic expectations usually have a damaging, disillusioning impact. How long will a high school track team remain motivated if their coach tells them that every student needs to run a mile fast enough to break the world record? Well, the unrealistic expectations embodied in NCLB are apt to have that same impact on America's teachers. Disillusioned teachers—teachers labeled as ineffective—are not likely to provide the best possible education for our nation's children.

Until more realistic AYP timeline expectations have been mandated by federal lawmakers, my best advice to state-level decision makers is to install an NCLB accountability system that is (1) most likely to produce accurate per-school evaluations, (2) most likely to stimulate improved classroom instruction, and (3) least likely to cause educational harm to students. Throughout this book, I have described the key elements that need to be included in such an NCLB-based accountability program. If you share my views, and even if you find my prediction reasonable that AYP timelines will be modified in the future, it is still possible for you to do something *now* in your own state to see that schools are evaluated as appropriately as possible. This is truly a moment when activism is needed.

It is easy to read a book such as this, then do nothing. It is easy to conclude that "doing something" should be left to others. But in our nation's schools, NCLB has created a situation in which way too many children are now at risk. If you're an educator, then this law is likely to give you and your colleagues an unwarranted black eye. Do something about it. If you're a parent, your child's education is most likely going to be tarnished because of this law. Do something about it. If nothing is done to make No Child Left Behind benefit children, it won't.

Additional Reading

PUBLICATIONS

Anderson, Lorin W. and Sid F. Bourke. *Assessing Affective Characteristics in the Schools.* 2d ed. Mahwah, N.J.: Lawrence Erlbaum Associates, 2000.

This practical account of how educators ought to go about measuring students' affective dispositions is the second edition of a book published originally in 1981. This excellent book, clearly understandable to non-educators, may interest those readers who want to dig more deeply into affective assessment than the summary I provided here.

Chappuis, Jan and Stephen Chappuis. *Understanding School Assessment.* Portland, Ore.: Assessment Training Institute, 2002.

This book deals with classroom assessment rather than the sorts of large-scale standardized tests called for by NCLB. Three topics, however, will prove particularly informative to parents regarding such classroom testing. The authors describe (1) the relationship between classroom assessment and students' motivation, (2) the decision makers who should rely on evidence supplied by classroom tests, and (3) the proper role of parents and community members related to classroom assessment.

Erpenbach, William J., Ellen Forte-Fast, and Abigail Potts. *Statewide Educational Accountability under NCLB.* Washington, D.C: Council of Chief of State School Officers, 2003.

In this booklet, the authors describe, in summary form, key issues reflected in the accountability plans that states have submitted for approval to federal officials. The authors' observations are particularly interesting, for there is considerable attention given areas in which states attempted to "push the envelope" when attempting to comply with NCLB and its attendant regulations. Although the analysis does not address states' standards or assessments, it is clear from this report that officials in many states are attempting to avoid the perception their public schools are performing badly.

Kohn, Alfie. *The Schools Our Children Deserve: Moving beyond Traditional Classrooms and "Tougher Standards."* Boston: Houghton Mifflin, 1999.

Kohn is one of this era's most outspoken critics of our nation's frequently flawed educational accountability programs. In this carefully researched volume, he sets forth a cogent argument about why the quest for "tougher standards" often stifles the sort of classroom experiences that we really want our students to have. Kohn puts forward a persuasive critique of the kinds of standardized tests now used so widely in the United States. In a subsequent, more concise book, *The Case against Standardized Testing* (Portsmouth, N.H.: Heinemann, 2000), the essentials of Kohn's quarrels with such tests are succinctly reiterated.

Lemann, Nicholas. *The Big Test.* New York: Farrar, Straus and Giroux, 1999.

Lemann's thought-provoking book provides an insightful historical commentary on the pivotal role that intelligence tests have played in the United States during the last half of the twentieth century, including the role of Educational Testing Service (ETS) in these events. Lemann points out how the function of ETS in promoting the widespread use of intelligence tests has, heretofore, not been widely recognized. The subtitle of the book accurately conveys its exposé nature: "The Secret History of the American Meritocracy."

Ohanian, Susan. *One Size Fits Few.* Portsmouth, N.H.: Heinemann, 1999.

A former teacher, Ohanian devotes this slender volume to a forceful casti-gation of the standards movement in American schools. She identifies numerous educational catastrophes that she contends spring directly from the misguided efforts of individuals who are too zealous in their promotion of students' standards mastery. Because of NCLB's heavy reli-ance on the precise sort of educational standards that Ohanian reviles, one can safely infer that she will be having difficulty with the manner in which many states have attempted to implement NCLB.

Popham, W. James. *Testing! Testing! What Every Parent Should Know about School Tests.* Boston: Allyn and Bacon, 2000.

Written immediately before enactment of NCLB, this book attempted to help parents understand educational tests in the pre-NCLB era of high-stakes testing. As research professor Ronald Berk of Johns Hopkins University commented, this book is a "must-read for all parents who want to understand the real meaning of their children's test scores."

Popham, W. James. *The Truth about Testing: An Educator's Call to Action.* Alexandria, Va.: Association for Supervision and Curriculum Development, 2001.

This book, written chiefly for educators and educational policy makers, deals with many of the same topics treated in the previous pages. It has been read by a good many American teachers and school administra-tors. Although the book is aimed at educators, parents will find its message relevant.

Popham, W. James. *Test Better, Teach Better: The Instructional Role of Assessment.* Alexandria, Va.: Association for Supervision and Curricu-lum Development, 2003.

Because many U.S. teachers have not taken coursework in educational assessment, this slender volume is intended to help both experienced and in-preparation teachers understand that well-conceived testing can contribute to better teaching. This book, of less interest to parents, provides a dollop of assessment literacy for educators.

Sacks, Peter. *Standardized Minds*. Cambridge, Mass.: Perseus, 1999.

Although focused on intelligence (aptitude) tests rather than achievement tests (the types of tests called for in NCLB), this carefully researched book provides a number of illuminating insights related to assessment. In one chapter, Sacks offers his view of educational accountability as "The Great American Dumb-Down: How the Accountability Machine Harms Schools." Sacks supplies a disturbing account of how tests were employed as a vehicle for "inventing intelligence during the previous century."

WEBSITE

At www.ioxassessment.com you will find a variety of assessment-related essays as well as descriptions of videotape and in-print materials for educators and parents. One product of particular relevance is a three-part videotape series, *The Trouble with Testing*, dealing with educational assessment. This PBS-quality series was produced by South Carolina Educational Television. Each of its three fifty-five-minute videotapes, ideal for airing on community TV stations, is also available in a sixteen-minute format suitable for at-home parent viewing.

Notes

1. "States Revise the Meaning of Proficient," *Education Week* 22, no. 6 (2002).
2. Popham, W. James, "The Debasement of Student Proficiency," *Education Week* 23, no. 16 (2003): 30.
3. Popham, W. James, "The 'No Child' Noose Tightens—But Some States Are Slipping It," *Education Week* 190, no. 2 (2003): 48.
4. These associations were the American Association of School Administrators; the National Association of Elementary School Principals; the National Association of Secondary School Principals; the National Education Association; and the National Middle School Association.
5. The members of the Commission on Instructionally Supportive Assessment were Eva L. Baker, University of California–Los Angeles; David C. Berliner, Arizona State University; Carol Camp Yeakey, University of Virginia; James W. Pellegrino, University of Illinois–Chicago; W. James Popham (chair), University of California–Los Angeles; Rachel F. Quenemoen, University of Minnesota; Flora V. Rodríguez-Brown, University of Illinois–Chicago; Paul D. Sandifer (Ret.), South Carolina Department of Education; Stephen G. Sireci, University of Massachusetts–Amherst; and Martha L. Thurlow, University of Minnesota.
6. These websites are www.aasa.org, www.naesp.org, www.principals.org, www.nea.org, and www.nmsa.org.